IF I ONLY KNEW THEN WHAT I KNOW NOW™

The Lessons of Life and What They're Trying to Teach You

Robert Wolff

Published by The Creative Syndicate

IF I ONLY KNEW THEN WHAT I KNOW NOW™

The Lessons of Life and What They're Trying to Teach You

Robert Wolff

Published by The Creative Syndicate
10400 Overland Road, Suite 143
Boise, Idaho, USA 83709

Copyediting by Lynette Smith
Book Interior Design by Betty Abrantes

Book Information: www.RobertWolff.com

Copyright © 1997–2012 by Robert Wolff
All Rights Reserved. No part of this book may be reproduced or transmitted in any form or by any means without written permission from the author. All trademarks are the exclusive property of the author.

Print edition ISBN: 978-1-937939-00-7
Electronic edition ISBN: 978-1-937939-01-4
First printing 2011
Library of Congress Control Number 2011961672

Note: Inspirational quotations not otherwise attributed were written by Robert Wolff.

INTRODUCTION

Ever since I can remember, I've loved watching people.

And for however brief or long any of them has been in my life, they have been my teachers and without them, I wouldn't be the person who I am.

Thank you.

For years, and without really much thought as to why, I kept reflecting on the experiences I had with people and the things I observed, as I daily looked forward to and enjoyed my interactions with those who traversed my world.

It was during my years living in California that I felt compelled to start writing down the things I had observed and the lessons I had learned from them.

These are the first of those lessons.

They touched my heart and impacted my life.

I hope they do the same for you.

With best wishes for your happiness and success,

Robert

CONTENTS

LESSON 1
Very Few People See Life as You Do ... 1

LESSON 2
Inside You Is a Voice That Is Always Calling You to Change ... 3

LESSON 3
We're Only Here for a Flicker ... 5

LESSON 4
Keep It Simple ... 7

LESSON 5
Do You Know a Good Thing When You See It? ... 9

LESSON 6
The Givers and the Takers ... 12

LESSON 7
The Change Will Do You Good ... 15

LESSON 8
Friends—Many Come and Many Go ... 17

LESSON 9
The Personal Inventory ... 20

LESSON 10
Throw a Little Seed Money ... 22

LESSON 11
Be a Kid Again ... 25

LESSON 12
It's Time to Catch a Glimpse ... 27

LESSON 13
Love, Relationships and the Art of Giving ... 30

LESSON 14
Life is Meant to Be Enjoyed, Not Endured ... 33

LESSON 15
Always Take Time to Play ... 36

LESSON 16
The Only Way You Will Ever Know
Is to Experience, as Only You Know, What's Best for You ... 39

LESSON 17
Always Have Lots of Projects ... 42

LESSON 18
Focus Your Energies on Things in Smaller Increments ... 45

LESSON 19
Expect Nothing But the Very Best ... 47

LESSON 20
Always Question Everything ... 50

LESSON 21
We're All the Same Except from the Neck Up 53

LESSON 22
What a Difference 24 Hours Makes 57

LESSON 23
A Half Hour Across the Table
from a Wise Man is Worth More than a Month's Study of Books 60

LESSON 24
You Don't Own Anything 62

LESSON 25
People Act Differently at Night 64

LESSON 26
You Can Always Do Things Much Better
and Faster than You Think You Can 67

LESSON 27
The Best Way to Learn Anything Is by Doing 69

LESSON 28
I Wish I Had What You Have 71

LESSON 29
The Sacredness of Feelings 73

LESSON 30
The Magnet of Attraction 75

LESSON 31
Take Control 79

LESSON 32
Don't Doubt What You Don't Hear 82

LESSON 33
Hold Yourself to a Higher Standard 85

LESSON 34
Your Life Is Exciting in Proportion to the
Number of Things You Have to Look Forward To 87

LESSON 35
People Are a Lot Like Animals: With Hurt or Pain
Comes a Deep Need to Be Left Alone 89

LESSON 36
No One Can Make You Upset Without Your Permission 91

LESSON 37
People Love the Underdog 94

LESSON 38
Never Do Anything You Can Pay Someone Else to Do Better than You 96

LESSON 39
Rich Is the Person Who Makes Their Income Fit the Lifestyle.
Poor Is the Person Who Makes their Lifestyle Fit their Income. ... 98

LESSON 40
Do the Things That Add to Your Happiness ... 100

LESSON 41
The Brain Drain ... 102

LESSON 42
Be Your Own Best Friend ... 105

LESSON 43
Keep Your Mind on the Things You Want
and Off the Things You Don't Want ... 108

LESSON 44
You Were Given Complete Unchallengeable Control
Over Just One Thing, and It's Called "Your Thoughts" ... 111

LESSON 45
Those with Big Faith Get Big Results ... 114

LESSON 46
The One-Uppers ... 116

LESSON 47
You Are a Mind with a Body ... 118

LESSON 48
Reveal What You Will for the Answer You Want ... 120

LESSON 49
You Don't Have to Be Anything Except Yourself ... 122

LESSON 50
Things Just Are ... 124

LESSON 51
There's Nothing Like Experiencing Something for the First Time ... 126

LESSON 52
Going Through Hard Times Makes You Appreciate the Good Times ... 129

LESSON 53
Take Good Care of Things ... 132

LESSON 54
The Only Pressure You Have Is That Which You Put on Yourself ... 134

LESSON 55
Assumption Is the Mother of Many Foul-Ups ... 136

LESSON 56
How Well Are You Trained? ... 138

LESSON 57
Is Your Life Another Dream That Ended Way Too Soon? ... 140

LESSON 58
Listen to What They Say They're Not,
Because That's Usually What They Are — 142

LESSON 59
It's Always a Good Time to Get Back to Basics — 145

LESSON 60
Whatever Happened to the Masters and the Masterpieces? — 148

LESSON 61
If It Isn't One Thing, It's Another — 150

LESSON 62
Oh, Those Questions — 152

LESSON 63
Watch Out for the Sheep — 155

LESSON 64
The Excuses for Not Being, Not Doing and Not Having — 157

LESSON 65
The Power and Emotion of a Handwritten Letter — 160

LESSON 66
Tell Me About Your Perfect Day — 162

LESSON 67
You Are Moving in the Direction of Your Pictures — 164

LESSON 68
The Body You Have Is the Body You Want — 166

LESSON 69
Is Your Life an "I Can't Wait to Get Over This" Event? — 168

LESSON 70
Circumstances? I Make My Own! — 171

LESSON 71
Balancing the Triangle — 173

LESSON 72
The Power of Forgiveness—It's Time to Set Yourself Free — 175

LESSON 73
Break Free from the Shackles of the Past — 177

LESSON 74
In Your Mind, There's No Space and Time — 180

LESSON 75
Your Parents Did the Best They Knew — 182

LESSON 76
You Learn by Watching — 184

LESSON 77
When It Comes to People, I'm Positive That Most Are Negative — 186

LESSON 78
Jealousy and Gossip, the World's Favorite Sports — 188

LESSON 79
You Can Become an Expert — 191

LESSON 80
The Give and Take of Love — 194

LESSON 81
Money Is the Root of Much Goodness — 196

LESSON 82
Get Plugged Back into Your Power Source — 199

LESSON 83
Paying Your Do's — 201

LESSON 84
The Lost Art of Listening — 203

LESSON 85
Mentors—Your Greatest Teachers — 206

LESSON 86
A Model for Success — 209

LESSON 87
Learning from the "Someday I'll," "If Only I Had" and "I Should Have" Experiences — 212

LESSON 88
Tell Me What You Want, Not What You Don't — 214

LESSON 89
The Power of Words — 216

LESSON 90
You Can Climb the Highest Mountain — 219

LESSON 91
If You Compare, Get Ready for Despair — 223

LESSON 92
You Were Designed to Create, Not Compete — 225

LESSON 93
Say Goodbye to the Assassins of Your Success and Happiness — 228

LESSON 94
The Power of an Organized Mind — 230

LESSON 95
Timing is Everything — 232

LESSON 96
Where Are All the Heroes? — 234

LESSON 97
Running Around in Circles — 236

LESSON 98
You Must First Give That Which You Wish to Receive — 239

LESSON 99
You Don't Know How Much You Affect Other People — 241

LESSON 100
Your Word Is Your Bond — 243

LESSON 101
The Courage to Stand Alone — 246

LESSON 102
The Power of Discipline — 248

LESSON 103
The Last Impression — 251

LESSON 104
It's What You Do that Determines the Kind of Life You'll Live — 254

LESSON 105
Become a Seeker of Truth — 256

LESSON 106
Life Is Experience — 259

LESSON 107
Experience Has Nothing to Do with Ability — 261

LESSON 108
Your Actions Say Who and What You Are and What You Believe — 264

LESSON 109
I Am Responsible — 267

LESSON 110
The Habit of Success — 270

LESSON 111
Make Sure to Break Fast — 272

LESSON 112
Give Everything Your Best — 274

LESSON 113
You Grow on the Journey — 275

LESSON 114
Get Focused Like a Laser Beam — 277

LESSON 115
Welcome to the University of Life — 280

LESSON 116
Ask for What You Want — 282

LESSON 117
Stop Majoring in Minor Things — 284

LESSON 118
Use the Power of Replacement — 285

LESSON 119
Life Is Like a Wave — 288

LESSON 120
Yearn to Learn — 290

LESSON 121
Know the Difference Between You and Your Body — 292

LESSON 122
Questions Can Change Your Life — 296

LESSON 123
The Hidden Agenda — 298

LESSON 124
In All Honesty — 300

LESSON 125
One of Life's Greatest Lessons — 302

LESSON 126
What You Believe Is What You Get — 304

LESSON 127
Out with the Old and In with the New — 307

LESSON 128
The Hidden Genie — 309

LESSON 129
You Have Never Failed — 314

LESSON 130
The Miracle that's Called "You" — 316

LESSON 131
Let's Open Your Owner's Manual — 319

LESSON 132
Everything in Life Happens for a Reason — 321

LESSON 133
You Will Catch More Flies with Honey than with Vinegar — 323

LESSON 134
Go Where Others Fear, and Life Will Meet You There with Rewards Others Can Only Dream About — 326

LESSON 135
Know When to Let Go — 328

LESSON 136
Become the Exceptional Person — 330

LESSON 137
See the Big Picture — 333

LESSON 138
The Big Chase — 336

LESSON 139
This Just In: It's Okay to Get Excited! ... 339

LESSON 140
Learn from Others' Mistakes,
Because You'll Never Live Long Enough to Make Them Yourself ... 341

LESSON 141
Choose Carefully Those from Whom You Seek Advice ... 344

LESSON 142
Yesterday's Success is Like Yesterday's News—Quickly Forgotten ... 346

LESSON 143 349
Getting Out of the Holding Pattern ... 348

LESSON 144
Thinking About Your Problem Won't Change It, But Action Will ... 350

LESSON 145
Time to Be the Rider and Not the Horse ... 352

LESSON 146
The World is Full of Talkers ... 355

LESSON 147
The Thing You Prepare for Is Often the Thing That Never Comes ... 356

LESSON 148
Tell Everyone What You're Going to Do, But First Show Them ... 359

LESSON 149
What You Own May Eventually Own You ... 361

LESSON 150
Things are Never Quite What They First Appear to Be ... 364

LESSON 151
You're Always Becoming a New Person ... 365

LESSON 152
Take What You Have and Get Started ... 368

LESSON 153
Open the Floodgates ... 370

LESSON 154
All You Need Is One Hit ... 373

LESSON 155
Take the Time and Get Away ... 375

LESSON 156
You're Never Too Old ... 378

LESSON 157
Desire Is the Force Behind All Things and Moves the World ... 381

LESSON 158
Your Environment Impacts Your Reality ... 383

LESSON 159
We Remember Most Those Who Were Hardest on Us ... 385

LESSON 160
Life is Made Up of Defining Moments ... 388

LESSON 161
Be Hard on Yourself at the Right Time ... 390

LESSON 162
Tear Down Your Fences ... 393

LESSON 163
Say What You Want ... 396

LESSON 164
The Images You Keep Playing in Your Mind
Keep Bringing You the Things You Have ... 400

LESSON 165
Time to Clean Out the Closet ... 403

LESSON 166
The Incredible Power of One ... 404

LESSON 167
Just Get in the Neighborhood ... 406

LESSON 168
Do the Things You Want to Do ... 409

LESSON 169
Plan Your Dreams on What You Want and Not on What You Have ... 413

LESSON 170
Go to the Water for Cleansing ... 415

LESSON 171
Why Be a Copy When You Can Be the Original? ... 418

LESSON 172
Never Rush God's Timing and His Plan for Your Life ... 421

LESSON 173
Always Have Passion and Romance for Everything You Do ... 423

LESSON 174
Be Still and Listen ... 426

LESSON 175
Change Your Expectations to Preferences ... 428

LESSON 176
A Preview of What Happpens as You Begin Living Your New Life ... 431

LESSON 177
The Walk with God ... 435

Share Your Life Lesson Story with the World ... 438

LESSON 1

VERY FEW PEOPLE SEE LIFE AS YOU DO

We are all born under the same sky, but we don't all have the same horizon.
—Konrad Adenaur

And my, how we want them to, and it can be downright frustrating that they don't.

Inside us, our true personality wants to come out, yet, there's no way we feel safe in allowing it to unless we feel that others really understand us, our world and what we're all about.

But, you know what? That's never going to happen, because each of us will see the same events and experiences differently.

But why?

Well, not only are each of our brains wired differently—that's right, even twins see events and remember experiences differently—but our filter which everything must first pass through is colored by our perceptions about what has happened to us in the past and what we have *chosen* to keep as important past reference for any future events that we might experience. Seems your brain is always looking for a past event to relate to whatever new experience it may be seeing and experiencing now.

Admit it: It's a wonderful feeling to believe our lives and relationships would be much richer if others could just step inside our bodies for only a brief few seconds to really feel those things we're feeling. To see the potential we see in a new project. To feel the excitement of what some great news may mean to our and their future. And to reminisce about a wonderful vacation we took and all the people and places we experienced and have them feel those same wonderful feelings.

THE LESSON TO BE LEARNED IS...

As much as we'd like, others will never totally understand us. The best you can do is understand the other person's reference system—do they describe their experiences in matter-of-fact words, pictures or emotions?—and then describe the things you want them know with the words, pictures or emotions they understand best. And have them do the same for you. Get on the same wavelength, be specific about your descriptions and what you want them to know. Doing that will have both of you speaking, feeling and understanding in each other's own language.

LESSON 2

INSIDE YOU IS A VOICE THAT IS ALWAYS CALLING YOU TO CHANGE

Be content with what you have;
never with what you are.
—B.C. Forbes

Just where in the heck does this voice come from?

Geez, I mean here you are, you've worked your tail off to get where you are and no sooner than you get there, there's that voice again, telling you to enjoy your success but don't get too comfortable, because soon it'll be time to change. But face it: You resist change because you're comfortable. It took you awhile to arrive where you are, but life feels good to you now. Yet inside of each of us, something pulls on our heartstrings that says, "Enjoy your success, but you can only stay here for a short time. Then it's time to move on and grow if you really want to be the great success you're designed to be."

Most people fear change. They want to see the result before they make any decision. Yet life doesn't work that way. So to keep their mind off change, they don't change their lives because they have found a way to take their minds off their own lives by getting caught up in others'.

Look around you. How many people do you know, hear or see who are so busy getting caught up in what's going on in other people's lives, living in the past or reacting to the events that life presents to them, that they keep their minds off their lives and what would truly give them deep fulfillment and happiness?

A lot!

Makes you wonder why so many great people have settled for so little when they can have so much. Why have they let their major purpose in life become worrying about others or just getting through the day by keeping their problems to a minimum? They tend to live by the creed of "maximum worry for minimum results." No wonder they're constantly frustrated and unhappy.

Know this: The desire for change is *always* knocking at your door. The question is, do you believe enough in yourself and your dreams to make life pay off, on your terms? Are you one of those rare people who lives the kind of life that makes you happiest? If not, begin asking yourself: Why are you afraid of change?

THE LESSON TO BE LEARNED IS...

Embrace the desire inside you to change, to grow, to learn, to experience and to be all you were meant to be. Change is good, very good. For the law of nature is either you grow or you die—there's no in-between. If you have the desire for change, it means you are alive! Embrace it and begin living your life in a big new way.

LESSON 3

WE'RE ONLY HERE FOR A FLICKER

I waited too long to start living.
—Anonymous

The older you get, the faster life seems to move.

I don't know how many times I've heard that, and you know it's true. Think back to when you were a kid. Things couldn't seem to happen quickly enough. Your first date, the day you got your drivers license, graduation—these and so many other events seemed to take forever until they finally came.

Then in your twenties, life seems to move a bit quicker, yet, you don't fully realize it because so much of your time is devoted to going to college, trying different jobs and finding a career, getting into a relationship and maybe building a family or deciding that traveling the world in search of fame, fortune, romance and adventure may be your calling. Seems that for each year after that, the years seem like days and hours seem like minutes.

When you're younger, it's easy to listen to others who tell you, "Why are you in such a hurry? Slow down, you've got plenty of time. You've got your whole life ahead of you?" The truth is, you do have your whole life ahead of you, but it's moving pretty quickly.

THE LESSON TO BE LEARNED IS…

Each and every day you are alive is a truly precious gift, and it's one that cannot be bought at any price. The richest person in the world, even with all that wealth, cannot buy an extra day of life. So be truly thankful for your gift of life. It was given to you for a very special reason.

Believe in yourself and make your dreams happen today. Dreams that will help inspire others and bring you deep happiness. Forget the excuses and lies you've allowed yourself to believe, that your dreams are only for others to achieve. They are *your* dreams, and you can make whatever you want happen.

The trap of thinking there will always be tomorrow will hold you back forever, and one day there won't be a tomorrow. It's just that none of us know when. You have no guarantee of tomorrow, and yesterday is gone and can never be brought back. All you have is *now*.

Each of us has 1,440 minutes in a single day. That's 168 hours in a week and 61,320 hours in a year. If you live to the wonderful age of 90—and let's hope it will be much longer!—you will have lived a total of 32,850 days on this earth.

If you're 30, you've lived 10,950 of those days; if you're 40, 14,600 days; if you're 50, 18,250 days. I think you're catching my drift. Those days are priceless and can never be repeated.

My friend, my question to you is, what are you doing with your priceless day today?

LESSON 4

KEEP IT SIMPLE

*Nothing is more simple than greatness;
indeed, to be simple is to be great.*
—Ralph Waldo Emerson

Why do we try to complicate things in life? Is it a quirk of human nature that says if something's easy, it must be wrong? Since when did struggle equate with significance of accomplishment?

For many people, the more complicated things are, the more anxiety and stress they feel and the more they feel out of control in their lives. This creates frustration, tension and unhappiness and prevents people from feeling the deep sense of calm they must have if they want to operate at their most creative best.

THE LESSON TO BE LEARNED IS…

Life is simple and so should yours be.

In nature and in your life, the simple is always the most powerful. Things don't need 16, 32 or 64 moving parts to be great. Look at music. There are only seven major notes. Yet, look how Beethoven Brahms, Handel, Vivaldi, Bach, Sinatra, Nat King Cole, Elvis, The Eagles, The Rolling Stones and every other musical artist before or after these people used and will use those seven notes to create masterpieces.

Begin to look for the simplicity in everything you do.

You're going to be amazed at how simple everything in your life can be, if only you will start to see it as such. Soon you will learn that simplicity and complexity are only a matter of perception.

How easy or difficult things appear is only a matter of your perception. Remember the age-old truth: Think of things as easy, and your mind will find ways to prove it so.

LESSON 5

DO YOU KNOW A GOOD THING WHEN YOU SEE IT?

Most human beings are unhappy either because of what they know or because of what they don't know. Ignorance remains bliss only so long as it is ignorance; as soon as one learns one is ignorant, one begins to want not to be so.

—Anonymous

Unfortunately, many people don't know a good thing when they see it.

How can they, when they've never really given it much thought? How many great people do you know who were employed by a company, only to have some boss or manager in that company view that great person as a threat? Filled with jealousy and a fragile ego, the boss or manager made it their mission to make this great person's work world a living hell, eventually forcing this person out because they were perceived as a threat.

Then there are relationships.

Have you ever been in a relationship with someone to whom you gave every bit of yourself to help make this person's life something truly wonderful and special; and even with all the love and attention you gave, it was not enough? They may even have told you that you were the best thing that ever happened to them, but eventually their actions—or inactions—were factors that helped end the relationship.

So what do both of these scenarios have in common? Both are examples of people's not knowing, allowing and fully experiencing a good thing when they see it.

You see, for so long, many people have lived their lives with limited beliefs and information as to what is really good. And the things they don't know are good are perceived as either bad or a threat and ultimately must be rejected.

For years, they've based so many of their choices on what they think they need. Not on what they really need, which is what comes with awareness.

THE LESSON TO BE LEARNED IS...

It is time to expand your awareness by deciding what you truly want.

Think about and ask yourself empowering and life-changing questions, wait for the answers and then act on them immediately.

For example: What kind of people would be good for you to have on your team to help you reach an important life goal?

What kind of people and experiences would empower you?

What kind of experiences and people would help fill your life with positive growth and joy?

Let go of what you think you need and want—based on what you've received and accepted in the past—and go for what you can experience and have right now.

The great news is, as your awareness expands, so will you ability to truly know a good thing when you see it.

| LIFE'S WORDS OF WISDOM |

*We would often be sorry
if our wishes were gratified.*

—Aesop

LESSON 6

THE GIVERS AND THE TAKERS

There is no happiness in having or getting, but only in giving.

—Henry Drummond

During your life, you will interact with basically two types of people: givers and takers. Which of these two groups of people you decide to spend your time with will determine just what kind of person you are.

Let's look at both.

THE TAKERS

A great deal of our world is filled with these kinds of people. These are the folks who expect you to do things for them. They expect to be treated nice. They expect you to run after them. They expect you to devote the majority of your conversation listening to them about what they have to say about themselves. They expect you to be interested in what's happening in their lives. They expect that you won't want much from them, because they don't feel like giving much.

And once you stop being interested in them, they become uninterested in you and move on to someone else who will give them the attention they crave.

THE GIVERS

Think of them as the rare group of people who are the most successful on the planet. Sure, some takers can be very successful, but their success lasts for only a short time. Not only that, they can never be truly happy or successful because they are so consumed by getting, that they never developed the mindset to give to others, help others and enjoy the success they have. These people have never learned one of the greatest laws of success: You must first give, before you can get.

The givers are those who freely give their time to help others become the best they can be. They don't see through others, they see others through. Whether it's good times or bad, the givers are there to help.

Givers are excellent listeners. They know most people will talk about themselves for much of the conversation, but that doesn't matter. Givers enjoy listening and learning. They seem to understand that our Creator gave us two ears and one mouth so we will listen twice as much as we talk.

Whenever givers speak, it's because they have something to say; a word of encouragement, a laugh to cheer others up. Their words are well placed and well intentioned, and they accomplish exactly what the giver wants them to.

THE LESSON TO BE LEARNED IS...

Remember the old saying, "Talking is sharing, but listening is caring." People will give you whatever it is you want, if they first know you care about them and are willing to help them. It is true that people don't care how much you know until they first know how much you care.

The motivational speaker Zig Ziglar said it best: "You can have everything in life you want if you will just help enough other people get what they want."

Being a giver is one wonderful way to do that.

LIFE'S WORDS OF WISDOM

*Ultimately nothing matters very much.
The defeat that seems to break your heart today
will be but a ripple among the waves of
other experiences in the ocean of your life
further ahead.*

—Anonymous

[IF I ONLY KNEW THEN WHAT I KNOW NOW™]

LESSON 7

THE CHANGE WILL DO YOU GOOD

*We are not creatures of circumstance;
we are creators of circumstance.*

—Benjamin Disraeli

How many times have you heard that "the change will do you good?" Friends, co-workers, family reaffirming that whatever change you may be going through in your life right now will be good for you.

At the time, you don't want to hear that. The uneasiness, pain and frustration you're feeling isn't comforted by words. The only thing that would help is to be over it, and quick.

The truth is you are changing every single day. The law of nature says either you grow or you die; there's no in-between.

Many people resist change because they are so unsure of the outcome. They want to know all the answers upfront, see every step that will be taken and know the final result, *before* they will act.

Yet, life doesn't work that way.

Life works by unchangeable law, faith and belief. You must have desire, belief and faith for great things in your life to happen, and then take focused action to ensure that they will.

THE LESSON TO BE LEARNED IS…

The Bible says that faith is the "substance of things hoped for and the conviction of things not seen." That means you don't have to *physically* see what you want to have or happen in order to have it or make it happen; you just have to have conviction and believe that it will. It's seeing a picture in your mind of your *already* having it.

Forget about the exact steps you'll take to get there, because they'll be vastly different from how you think you'll do it.

Look back at the kind of person you were 12 months ago.

Look at how much you've changed. Look at how much things in your life have changed. Amazing isn't it? You're not the same person you were 12 months ago, and you won't be the same person 12 months from now that you are today.

You're changing.

Every day, you're evolving to a brand new person each day.

That's exciting!

The old you of yesterday is nothing like the incredible you of today and the even greater person you'll be tomorrow.

Embrace change. Savor and enjoy it.

The best part of change is that you're the one who decides how you'll change. Change into the kind of person *you* want to become, never into what family, friends or society thinks you should become. Change your life so you are living the kind of life you dream of and truly want. Never, ever accept less from yourself.

:: The Lessons of Life and What They're Trying to Teach You ::

LESSON 8

FRIENDS—MANY COME AND MANY GO

No one is living aright unless he so lives that whoever meets him goes away more confident and joyous for the contact.
—Lilian Whiting

Throughout your life, you have met and will meet many people on your journey to where you're going.

Many of those friends will be good ones, but they may be a part of your life for only a short time. This brief friendship was necessary because both of you served a purpose. That purpose was to help and teach each other things you both needed to learn before you could move on to your next level and grow.

Many people don't understand that some friends are only transitory at best. They are in our lives for a short time, then gone.

Schoolmates and co-workers are two good examples. It seems that much frustration is caused when you try holding onto these friendships when it's time to let them go.

These friendships are like a beautiful butterfly that lands on our shoulder. We are changed and inspired by its beauty, but if we try to catch and hold it, it will fly away or be destroyed.

That's why you are to enjoy the moment, learn from it, let it impact your life and then let it move on to touch someone else's life.

You and I, we're just like that butterfly.

The truth is, we'll never know just how much and how many people's lives we've touched with the beauty of our friendships.

There are other friends who come into your life and fill a place that's been empty, as if this special person was placed in your life at just the right time to fill that emptiness. You enjoy being with them whenever you can and, like your favorite pair of old jeans or boots, these special friends just feel good and fit well.

These friends know you almost as well as you know yourself. They accept you totally the way you are without even a hint of trying to change you. They stick by your side through thick and thin, good times and bad. You can depend on them just as surely as you can depend on morning's following night.

THE LESSON TO BE LEARNED IS…

Know when to let go. Don't hold onto a memory or fall in love with what could be or someone's potential if deep down, you know it's not going to happen.

You'll know when you've got the kind of friendship or relationship that's built for the long term. Everything will just seem to click. You'll be able to totally be yourself and will always look forward to the time when you and your friend will be together.

Embrace all your friendships, however brief or long they may be. For contained within each is a gift and lessons you cannot experience anywhere else.

LIFE'S WORDS OF WISDOM

The life which is unexamined is not worth living.

—Plato

LESSON 9

THE PERSONAL INVENTORY

*It isn't lack of time that holds us back,
it's lack of direction.*

—Zig Ziglar

Take a look at your life, the things you've accomplished and the things you want to accomplish. Take a good look at where you are and where you want to be.

You may be surprised to learn that one of the biggest reasons you haven't accomplished more, experienced more, or enjoyed more is because you've been a time waster.

Ask yourself if the majority of your free time has been filled with activities that were tension relieving or goal achieving.

The truth is that lack of time usually means lack of direction. People have chosen to spend so much of their time majoring in minor things that they waste their precious time and life.

Look at your life. Think back to how many precious minutes, hours, days, months and years you have wasted simply because you've wasted time.

Think back to whenever you were getting ready for a vacation and you had an incredible amount of work and chores to accomplish. Those days before the vacation, it seemed like you'd never get all those things done.

Ah, but what always happened?

You always seemed to accomplish the seemingly

impossible, didn't you? And that's because you were focused and you gave your mind a clear goal and target to accomplish. In essence, you were making the ideal use of your time.

THE LESSON TO BE LEARNED IS…

Regardless of how busy you think you are, you will always find time to do the things that are important to you at that time in your life. While you may have lots of interests, you always find time to do the things you desire.

Remember, interest and desire are two very different things.

Lack of focus in knowing exactly what it is you want to achieve is one of the greatest reasons you waste time. The more locked in you are, and believe that you can achieve any goal you set your mind to, will all but eliminate the needless waste of the most precious resource you will ever have… time.

Tell yourself right now that you can use and indeed *want* to use every minute of every day to the fullest. It's a great feeling to be able to look in the mirror each night before bed and honestly tell yourself that you've made the most of the gift you've been given.

[IF I ONLY KNEW THEN WHAT I KNOW NOW™]

LESSON 10

THROW A LITTLE SEED MONEY

Those only are happy who have their minds fixed on some object other than their own happiness: on the happiness of others, on the improvement of mankind.
—John Stuart Mill

The most successful people in life understand and embrace something known as tithing and seed money.

The essence of tithing goes back many thousands of years when people would give to the government or churches a portion of their harvest or income. Ideally, this was done as a way of being thankful for the gifts, blessings and prosperity they and their families experienced.

Still, others took the tithing idea one step further by doing something called throwing seed money. Of course, you really don't throw it, you simply find someone who you may or may not know and give them something you have no intention of getting back.

This may mean money, clothes, books, food, your services or anything else you can think of that will help them over their obstacle in life and help them get on the road to success. The only repayment you require is that the person you helped will do the same for someone else down the road.

THE LESSON TO BE LEARNED IS…

We've all gone through tough times. Maybe you or someone you know is going through them right now. Just know this: Those tough times won't last long; they'll be over with very soon.

The quickest and best way to get over your own problem is to find someone else and help them to get over theirs.

But get ready. Tithing and throwing seed money will bring you rewards far greater than you might expect.

Seems that nature has set up a law that rewards those who help others and it does so in disproportion to the amount that was given. That is, you always get more in return than you give out.

Of course, the purpose is not for you to always be thinking about what you might get.

But be assured, whether it comes in love, money, opportunity or just plain wonderful feelings that you've made a big impact in someone's life, throwing seed money is something you'll never want to stop doing.

| LIFE'S WORDS OF WISDOM |

*We do not stop playing because we grow old;
we grow old because we stop playing.*

—Anonymous

LESSON 11

BE A KID AGAIN

The great man is he who does not lose his child's heart.
—Mencius

Inside of each of us is the deep desire and need to be a kid again.

Forget your age; it makes no difference. *All* of us have that child inside of us that begs to come out.

So why don't we let it?

Well, like sheep, many people believe they have to conform to how family, friends and society believe they should be or act. After all, acceptance is a greater need than happiness, right?

Makes you wonder why so many people live their lives through the disapproving smiles of others.

Little kids are so incredible.

They haven't learned to accept the negative limitations that others try to place on their every move.

They don't know what it's like to not trust and feel totally safe and comfortable doing whatever they want, whenever they want.

They can look you straight into the eyes and not say a word; yet my, how they cause people to look away because holding eye contact that long without saying a word is something society has taught us not to do.

THE LESSON TO BE LEARNED IS...

For you to be truly happy and content, you need to allow your true personality—the one who wants to be a child—to come out, whenever, wherever and as often as it wants.

It's time to quit suppressing that someone who's you!

Stop spending time with people who criticize and scrutinize you. They're the ones who won't dare let their little kid inside of them come out. These are the folks who will only pull you down and keep you frustrated.

Let the kid who made you smile, laugh, believe, dream big dreams and knew only possibilities and not problems, come out again.

It's that kid inside you who made you someone you really liked and who you never wanted to forget.

LESSON 12

IT'S TIME TO CATCH A GLIMPSE

Nothing in life is more exciting and rewarding than the sudden flash of insight that leaves you a changed person, not only changed, but for the better.
—Arthur Gordon

Have you ever experienced or looked at something, if only for a brief moment, and immediately what you experienced or what you saw registered in your mind as something important that you may or may not have wanted in your life?

For example, maybe you noticed the way someone treated their significant other in public; a touch of their hand on the back or the running of their hands through the other's hair might have triggered something inside you that reaffirmed what you'd like to experience in your own current or future relationship.

Seems that when your mind is trying to figure out some vague picture or feeling you've been giving it about something you want or something important to you, it will present to you those things in everyday life that cause you to look at them and say, yes or no, this is what I want or don't want.

In a sense, it's like a best friend (your subconscious mind) who could give you whatever you want asking you, if it (the subconscious mind) is on the right track to bring you what you really want.

THE LESSON TO BE LEARNED IS…

Get in touch and listen to your gut feeling and intuition whenever you experience things or feelings about something that's important to you.

Many times, they'll come very quickly and you may not even give them much thought, but they are powerful messengers that seek answers so they can help you have what you deeply desire and avoid that which you don't.

| LIFE'S WORDS OF WISDOM |

Life is to be in relations.

—Lao-Tzu

LESSON 13

LOVE, RELATIONSHIPS AND THE ART OF GIVING

Every year I live I am more convinced that the waste of life lies in the love we have not given, the powers we have not used, the selfish prudence that will risk nothing, and which, shirking pain, misses happiness as well. No one ever yet was the poorer in the long run for having once in a lifetime 'let out all the length of the reins.'

—Mary Cholmondeley

Many times in life, we'll go the extra mile and give, give, give and not receive the reward or gratitude we had hoped to receive from the person we had given to. Of course, there could be many reasons for this. Among them...

Maybe our expectations were too high. That is, from that particular person or from that particular person at that particular time. Quite possibly, with someone else, it could have been very different.

Maybe we gave for the wrong reasons, possibly by wanting to receive something intensely and immediately pleasurable to relieve our long-term loneliness, discomfort and pain.

But you know one of the strangest things in life is that life operates by unchanging law of cause and effect. It is absolutely unchangeable truth: "What you sow, so also shall you reap." In other words, what you give out has, must and will come back to you, and very often, many times multiplied with interest.

THE LESSON TO BE LEARNED IS…

One of the strangest things about this whole giving thing is that many times your reward won't come back to you from the person you first gave to and hoped to receive from.

No, many times it comes back to you from someone unexpected and who fits into the divine plan and perfect order for your life.

So many times we'll pour our heart and soul out to someone we start or want to start caring about and give them so much. Yet, many times they won't even acknowledge or deeply appreciate or fully comprehend what we've done for them.

Yet, we know, feel and believe deep down inside, that if someone would do something similar for us, we'd want to be with that person more. We'd want to share great things with them and really take an interest in their lives and want to know them better.

But we give up too soon and stop giving because we haven't received that something (or those somethings) in our "pre-set" and "pre-determined" time period or we haven't received what we want the way we think we should receive it. As a result, we get frustrated.

The fact is, the person we've given to may be going through so much in their lives at that time, maybe they're just numb to the whole thing. Your kindness and sincerity blows them away and, in a real sense, overwhelms them.

They know inside their heart that they must first take care of clearing up the cobwebs in their life, before they can fully appreciate and understand the kind of truly incredible person you are. *Then* they'll be able to begin to fully understand, enjoy, appreciate and cherish all the actions and all its meanings that you've given and are capable of.

It is only then that you can get the kind of response—and perhaps even greater response—you didn't expect from that very person whom you first may have thought was so cold.

And what if you don't?

No big deal.

Life's got you covered.

You're going to get it from someone else.

LESSON 14

LIFE IS MEANT TO BE ENJOYED, NOT ENDURED

*Very little is needed to make a happy life.
It is all within yourself, in your way of thinking.*
—Marcus Aurelius

Since when was life meant to be a struggle, difficult and not enjoyable?

You see, many people get a sense of satisfaction and reward from struggle. Somewhere inside, they have this belief that by being upset and believing that life is hard, they'll somehow get a greater reward down the road. After all, they see their friends, family and co-workers going through it on a daily basis, so it must be true; right?

Absolutely not.

THE LESSON TO BE LEARNED IS…

Make life pay off, on your own terms.

Remember this: you can have anything in life you truly desire, as long as you give up the belief that you can't have it.

Begin to see your life as a game—a fun game—that each day is filled with wonderful experiences to learn from.

See yourself using each experience to help you grow and become bigger, better and more in control of your life and helping you to achieve whatever it is you truly desire.

Remember that many people are upset at life because they never really understood the meaning behind the wise old saying…

Rich is the person who makes their income fit their lifestyle.

Poor [and let's also say frustrated] is the person who makes their lifestyle fit their income.

LIFE'S WORDS OF WISDOM

I do not know what I may appear to the world, but to myself I seem to have only been like a boy playing on the seashore, and diverting myself in now and then finding a prettier shell, or smoother pebble than ordinary, whilst the great ocean of truth lay all undiscovered before me.

—Sir Isaac Newton

LESSON 15

ALWAYS TAKE TIME TO PLAY

You can discover more about a person in an hour of play than in one year of conversation.
—Plato

So many folks are so caught up in having material things, accolades and worldly success that they've neglected a big part of their lives: play.

All work and little play makes for a very dull and boring life. You need an equal balance of work and play in order to release stress, tensions and pent-up energies that seek expression through ways other than just work.

THE LESSON TO BE LEARNED IS...

Look at some of the most successful people in life.

Yes, a few of them do nothing but work, work, work. To them, it's their life, the only thing they know. Yet I've known many of them—each worth hundreds of millions of dollars—and they feel like they can't stop. Like an addiction that if they stop to enjoy a hobby or play, their whole world would fall apart. Talk about being chronically frustrated and deeply unhappy!

Still, I've met many—measured in society's terms—worth infinitely more. They have found that taking time to play not only fulfills that deep inner need that constantly longs to be fulfilled, but the skills and discipline they learn through play actually helps them become better in their work.

What a beautiful benefit, and it's one you can start enjoying right now!

| LIFE'S WORDS OF WISDOM |

*Do the thing you fear
and the death of fear is certain.*

—Ralph Waldo Emerson

[IF I ONLY KNEW THEN WHAT I KNOW NOW™]

LESSON 16

THE ONLY WAY YOU WILL EVER KNOW IS TO EXPERIENCE, AS ONLY YOU KNOW, WHAT'S BEST FOR YOU

As soon as you trust yourself, you will know how to live.
—Johann Wolfgang Von Goethe

Have you ever wanted to take a trip to someplace you've never been before, dreamed of doing something you've always wanted to do yet never have, or been interested in a job and asked someone doing it how it was?

Of course you have.

And if you asked three different people who've done and experienced the same things, I'll bet that each of them gave you a different answer. And instead of helping you, their answers left you only more confused.

That's understandable.

You see, you and I and everyone else can see exactly the same thing, at the same time, and yet see, feel and describe very different things—all because of our perceptions.

Always remember whenever you ask others their opinions about direction for your life, they will only be able to see and feel things through *their* reference system based on *their* past experiences. And those experiences are never exactly what you have gone through, are going through or will go through.

Listen to *your* internal guidance system—your gut feeling and your conscience—because it knows the exact answer at the exact time for only you.

In this life, there's no way to really know how something will be until you experience it.

While we may ask others all kinds of questions in hopes of finding out, each one we ask has their own filter they use to pass judgment. So what you're getting is a distorted view of what something really is, based on the experiences of others and not yourself. Yet, so many people get hung up on devoting their quest to asking, that they never take the step and actually find out what that answer is for them. Perception is what comes out for us to remember after all those experiences have been filtered through our minds.

THE LESSON TO BE LEARNED IS...

The only way you will ever find the answers you seek to those questions or experiences you truly desire is to experience it for yourself.

Think back to when you were a kid.

Parents, in their hopes of being good parents and protecting their kids, often become too disciplined and overly protective so that their children won't make mistakes or suffer hurt.

Yet, what always happens? The children will go ahead and do it anyway because of the need to experience and find answers for themselves.

And this deep human craving to "find out for ourselves" doesn't stop after we get older. The craving is inherent; it's almost as if it is in our DNA, and is satisfied only by experiencing whatever it is that you desire yourself.

Yes, while it can be wise to listen to others—especially in matters of life or death—follow your intuition and call from within to experience that which you truly want.

Only then will you find the answers you seek.

LESSON 17

ALWAYS HAVE LOTS OF PROJECTS

A wise man will make more opportunity than he finds.

—Francis Bacon

Not only does it keep life exciting, it's a great way for you to make a lot of money.

Think of it like this: Many doctors make a lot of money. But their wealth depends basically on three things; how many patients they see, how many procedures they perform and how many hours they work. The fourth and fifth variables could be how many offices they open and how many people (other doctors) they have working for them.

The great news is that you don't have to be a doctor to be wealthy or live a life of excitement. By using your own unique, incredible creative powers, you can have any kind of life you want if you'll only create enough projects that will help other people.

THE LESSON TO BE LEARNED IS...

Strength is in numbers, and the greater the number of projects you're involved in, the greater the chances for your success.

You see, if you put all your energies into only one thing, your whole emotional being is wrapped up in that thing. Your future plans, financial future and how you feel about yourself creatively and successfully is tied up into making that one project pay off the way you've been dreaming and planning it would.

However, many times things don't happen like you dreamed and planned they would. So what happens? If you've only got one thing, it's a tremendous letdown and can drain you for days or even longer.

Yet, if you have many things going on at once, you have power. That's because if one thing doesn't work out, it's no problem because you've got five others that will.

Truly your life is exciting in proportion to the number of things you have to look forward to, and having lots of projects going keeps your life exciting. You'll also realize and fully appreciate that your opportunities and income in life are dependent not on how many hours you work, but on how many projects you create.

LIFE'S WORDS OF WISDOM

*Banish the future; live only for
the hour and its allotted work.
Think not of the amount of work
to be accomplished, the difficulties
to be overcome, but set earnestly at the
little task at your elbow, letting
that be sufficient for the day.*

—Osler

[IF I ONLY KNEW THEN WHAT I KNOW NOW™]

LESSON 18

FOCUS YOUR ENERGIES ON THINGS IN SMALLER INCREMENTS

Our grand business in life is not to see what lies dimly at a distance, but to do what lies clearly at hand.
—Thomas Carlyle

And speaking of creative projects, the key to being successful in those is separating which are 30–60–90 days and beyond.

Here's what I mean.

Writing a book may be a real passion for you. By all means, do it. However, by the time you finish writing that book and have it ready for others to buy and read, there can be quite a lag time if you do it through a traditional major publisher, and a much shorter lag time if you self-publish.

However, whichever you choose, there will still be a period of time between writing, completing and distributing it.

THE LESSON TO BE LEARNED IS...

While you're writing that best-seller, the wise course of action would be to create projects that will bring you income in the next 30 days, 60 days, 90 days and beyond.

Of course, stay focused on your long-term goals, but think of the future now by doing creative projects today that will help you reach your long-term objectives tomorrow.

| LIFE'S WORDS OF WISDOM |

If you advance confidently in the direction of your dreams and endeavor to live the life you have imagined, you will meet with a success unexpected in common hours.

—Henry David Thoreau

[IF I ONLY KNEW THEN WHAT I KNOW NOW™]

LESSON 19

EXPECT NOTHING BUT THE VERY BEST

It's a funny thing about life; if you refuse to accept anything but the best, you very often get it.
—W. Somerset Maugham

One of the biggest disappointments in life is expectation. For rare it is, that things in our lives exceed our expectations. When they do, it can be heavenly.

Think about it. How many times have you expected someone to treat you a certain way and they didn't? Or perhaps hope to have an experience turn out the way you expected it to, and things ended going in the totally opposite direction?

Don't sweat it, we all have. And you know it can be a real downer if we let it. After all, we had so much tied up into making what we expected turn out the way we thought it should. But people and life aren't like that.

THE LESSON TO BE LEARNED IS…

Forget expecting anything to happen in the exact way you think it should. People don't respond that way. And who says your way is the best way, anyhow, just because you may think it is?

The most enjoyable course to take is just to experience the moment.

Enjoy the people and experiences that come your way as something incredibly unique, one-of-a-kind and special, and meant to bring much depth and meaning to your life.

There is one truth about expectations that you can be absolutely sure of: Expect the best and get ready to experience it.

| LIFE'S WORDS OF WISDOM |

Some men see things as they are and ask why. Others dream things that never were and ask why not.

—George Bernard Shaw

[IF I ONLY KNEW THEN WHAT I KNOW NOW™]

LESSON 20

ALWAYS QUESTION EVERYTHING

If everyone is thinking alike, then no one is thinking.
—Benjamin Franklin

Have you ever watched a herd of sheep? All day long they follow the others without questioning (can animals question?) what or why they are doing what they're doing or where they are going.

That's kind of silly, isn't it?

Yet how silly do you think it is that many people you meet are just like sheep, blindly accepting what they're told by friends, family and society without using the most amazing machine ever created: their brain?

THE LESSON TO BE LEARNED IS…

Question everything in your life.

Why do you believe the things you do about people, religion, music, the arts, politics, food, relationships, animals, children and everything else?

You see, as humans, we love to have answers for just about everything. Even though those answers may not have been our own that we've taken time to think about and formulate, we still want answers to categorize people and things.

Yep, that labeling and category thing is a big deal for people.

You change your life in a hurry by asking yourself questions. The better the question, the better the answer, and the quicker you will have the information you need to move to the next level in your life.

Think back to an old love relationship that went sour.

While you were in the relationship, you believed everything was great. Then, for one reason or another, things changed and eventually you both parted. However, think of those great questions you asked yourself *after* the relationship was over. You know, questions like when was the first sign that something was going wrong? Why did I stay in it so long? What words or actions did the other do to tip me off that trouble was ahead?

Those were the kinds of questions that gave you excellent answers in a hurry that opened your eyes—maybe for the first time—that what you've been looking for and accepting in a relationship was something that's always brought you heartache and disappointment.

By getting answers to the questions you've asked yourself, you're in a much better place to finally have the experiences and relationship you truly want and deserve.

Question everything.

You'll be amazed at the answers you're going to get.

| LIFE'S WORDS OF WISDOM |

Every man is where he is by the law of his being. The thoughts which he has built into his character have brought him there, and in the arrangement of life, there is no element of chance, but all is the result of a law which cannot err.

—James Allen

[IF I ONLY KNEW THEN WHAT I KNOW NOW™]

LESSON 21

WE'RE ALL THE SAME EXCEPT FROM THE NECK UP

My mother said to me, 'If you become a soldier you'll be a general; if you become a monk you'll end up as the pope.' Instead, I became a painter and wound up as Picasso.
—Pablo Picasso

I'd like to share with you an experience that totally changed my life for the best, and I think reading about it will inspire you too.

I had the opportunity to live in Japan for about eight months. During that time, I met a man who was multi-billionaire.

On two occasions, I had the rare opportunity to visit with this man at one of his villas in Kyoto, Japan. The place was beautiful—as you can imagine it would be for a man worth billions—but the real beauty was hidden.

Inside the basement of one of his homes was an art gallery filled with many of the rarest paintings and art in the world. Monet, Picasso, Rembrandt, Buffet, Dali and many others—all bought by this man and his father. The paintings were easily worth tens of millions of dollars.

During one of my visits, I was invited to a tea ceremony with this rich man. With just the two of us—along with the tea server and translator—one of life's greatest lessons was about to be learned.

As I stood inches from this man and looked at him and all his great wealth and success, I asked myself, why was this man so incredibly successful?

Was he *that* different from everybody else?

Physically, no.

Mentally, yes.

For the first time, I realized he and I were similar.

We both had two arms and two legs, two eyes, two ears and one mouth.

Sure, I was taller than him by at least a foot and had to outweigh him by more than 100 pounds.

I was younger, faster and stronger.

Still, I kept asking myself, why is this man so successful when most others aren't?

Then it hit me.

The reason he's a billionaire and living the kind of extraordinary life most others will only dream of is because he's different from the neck up.

More specifically… from the eyes up.

His thoughts and beliefs are different from those of all others.

He never put any limits on his income; he never saw himself as only a 40-, 50- or 100–thousand-dollar-a-year person.

He believed he was worthy of experiencing fabulous opportunities and accomplishments and, as a result, his experiences and success have been and continue to be truly unlimited.

Yes, like any other human, he faced times of fear, doubt and heartache that could shake the very belief right out of a person.

Yet the big difference was, he never gave into to those fears and doubts or accepted them as major deciding factors and influences in his life.

His belief in himself overcame all those things that have held and continue to hold other people back from having and experiencing everything that's available to them right now.

THE LESSON TO BE LEARNED IS...

If I told you that I'd give you two million dollars but you wouldn't be able to use your legs, would you take the money?

Okay, what if I said I'd give you another two million dollars, but you wouldn't be able to use your arms again; would you take the money?

I'm betting you said no to both questions.

And you know what? You're already worth four million dollars and I'm just getting started.

The point I want to make is that you're already worth a fortune.

Your success and the kind of life you can have right now are beyond anything you've ever dreamed of. That's why I want you to start dreaming it and seeing yourself having that kind of life *right now.*

You've got to dream it, see it and believe yourself as having that kind of life before your mind will accept it as your reality and pull you irresistibly to that which you're picturing and believing.

You and that billionaire in Japan are no different from each other, from the eyes on down.

You're both human beings.

The *only* difference is in your thoughts and beliefs.

For if you will truly believe, as that man has, that you can have, be and do whatever it is you want—and you can have, be and do every single one of those things *right now*—you will absolutely experience it.

Just ask the billionaire who's living it.

LESSON 22

WHAT A DIFFERENCE 24 HOURS MAKES

When you get into a tight place and everything goes against you, till it seems as though you could not hold on a minute longer, never give up then, for that is just the place and time that the tide will turn.

—Harriet Beecher Stowe

Twenty-four hours is all it takes to change your life.

Do you believe that? It's absolutely true.

Think back to a moment when you were struggling. Maybe you were hit with unexpected bills or a job change. Maybe you broke up with an old lover or met a new one, or you put money down on a new car or a house. Whatever it was, that 24-hour period reshaped your life from that moment on.

Many times, we'll think our present situation is the only one we'll be in, so we adjust our thinking—almost like thinking, "Okay, this is what I'm going to be experiencing for awhile, so I'd better get used to it"—then suddenly things change.

That big business deal comes through. You get a raise, a new job, or a new opportunity is presented to you. Suddenly, in just 24 hours, your life is changed. The bills are paid. Your income goes up. The doctor gives you great news about concerns you had about your own health or that of a loved one. All within 24 hours.

THE LESSON TO BE LEARNED IS…

Always know that your life is changing every single day.

You are not the same today as you were yesterday, nor will you be the same tomorrow. Sure, your body may look the same, but inside, big time changes are going on.

Each day, you're growing mentally and spiritually and learning new lessons about yourself and the people and the events in the world you live in.

Change is great. In fact, if you weren't changing all the time, your life would be like this forever.

Always remember that the next 24 hours can change your life forever and for the best, if you will allow it to.

Those things that have been weighing heavy on your mind for so long can be lifted today. Along with that comes the incredible feeling that your life can different, better and filled with possibilities and not problems.

Live your life to the fullest today, but always be excited and look forward to tomorrow. Because in 24 hours, your life could change in wonderful ways you may never have dreamed possible.

| LIFE'S WORDS OF WISDOM |

*Many receive advice,
only the wise profit from it.*

—Publilius Syrus

LESSON 23

A HALF HOUR ACROSS THE TABLE FROM A WISE MAN IS WORTH MORE THAN A MONTH'S STUDY OF BOOKS

Sell your cleverness and buy bewilderment.
—Rumi

One of the fastest and most influential ways to change your beliefs and the direction of your life is to speak to a wise man or woman.

At different times in your life, people come into your life to teach you lessons you must learn before you're able to move to the next level of your growth. The old saying, "When the student is ready, the teacher will appear," is so true.

Sometimes we seek inspiration from books and people we may hear about on the Web, radio or television. But the real inspiration, the lasting inspiration, comes from those people who can relate to where we are in our lives, what we've been through or may be going through, and who can guide us and give us the answers and direction we seek; wise people whose words and actions help us to see that our problems and questions are not uniquely our own, and that for every question, there's an answer that's perfect for us.

:: The Lessons of Life and What They're Trying to Teach You ::

THE LESSON TO BE LEARNED IS…

Put away the false pride that keeps telling you that you know all the answers and don't need the inspiration from a wise person other than yourself.

Keep yourself open to each person who comes into your life, because each person can teach you something about yourself that you've been seeking answers to. Ask questions; for the better the question, the better the answer and the faster you can change your life.

You will be amazed at how easy it is to talk to successful people. The very people you may have always thought were way out of your league and wouldn't give you the time of day in fact are ready and willing to help.

There's something inside each of us that pulls us in the direction of helping others as we become more successful and fulfilled. Seems that the more successful someone is, the more they want to help and give back to others for the blessings they have received.

But be careful of those to whom you ask advice or reveal your dreams.

For many, if you tell your family and friends you want to own your own business, become a millionaire and be financially independent, build a beautiful dream home and travel the world, they'll look at you with disapproval and disbelief.

However, tell those same dreams to a wise person, a successful person, and they'll tell you how they did it and how you can too.

Talk about inspiration.

LESSON 24

YOU DON'T OWN ANYTHING

Know the three big lies: What I don't have is better than what I've got. More is always better. I'll be happy when I finally get what I want.

—Anonymous

You really don't own anything in this life. You're only using it.

Think about it. Everything you have—your money, car, home, clothes, jewelry, appliances—are things you use while you're here on this earth. And you take none of it with you once you're gone.

So why is it that so many people get freaked out if they lose a ring or the new car gets a ding? Many people let the drive to acquire and preserve material possessions rule their attitudes and lives. So much of who they are and how happy they are is related to how much they can get and how much they can keep.

And for what?

So they can work longer hours? Spend less time with their children? Be frustrated with all the bills that won't go away? And ignore their friends, family and loved ones because of the sacrifices they must make to pay for it all? Does that sound like a great life to you?

THE LESSON TO BE LEARNED IS...

If you're not careful, whatever you own will eventually own you and dictate your life. And, really, isn't your life worth more than just working long hours at a job where you're unfulfilled, just so you can pay bills and have things?

You're not going to take a single thing you're working so long and hard to own with you, when the candle of your life goes out.

Sure, it's great to enjoy the fruits of your labors and success, but to do so in exchange for worry, tension, and anxiety is a heavy price to pay for something you can't keep.

Freedom and a huge sense of relief come when you realize that you never truly "own" anything. It's time to start feeling good today.

[IF I ONLY KNEW THEN WHAT I KNOW NOW™]

LESSON 25

PEOPLE ACT DIFFERENTLY AT NIGHT

*The heights by great men reached and kept
were not attained by sudden flight,
but they, while their companions slept,
were toiling upward in the night.*

—Henry Wadsworth Longfellow

Ever wonder why so many crimes and wild behavior happens at night? It's almost as if some folks become unchained and the person they become is very different from who they are during the day.

For a lot of people, their actions at night stem from a sense of frustration with their lives and the direction they are going.

Their lack of belief in themselves and their ability to make whatever kind of life they dream of truly happen, causes many of them to rob, steal, do drugs and abuse themselves and others. And much of it with the hidden goal to do one thing: Change the way they feel about themselves, if only for a little while.

THE LESSON TO BE LEARNED IS...

The night has a way of hiding us and our behavior from others, but never from ourselves. It is always there, staring us in the face, 24 hours a day, seven days a week, 365 days a year.

Whatever it is we resist, really does persist, unless we face up to the truth: If something is bringing us pain, the only way it will go away is if we change our attitude toward it. That is, if we decide to keep it in our lives or get rid of it and find a better thing or experience to have.

Remember that night is still the other half of that same day.

Set your goals, see yourself as already having reached your goals, feel yourself experiencing the great feelings from reaching those goals. See and feel your life changing because you are making it the kind of life you've always wanted.

If you will do that, your nights will become like mornings—always filled with a new hope that something incredible is about to happen to you today.

| LIFE'S WORDS OF WISDOM |

Excellence is an art won by training and habituation. We do not act rightly because we have virtue or excellence, but we rather have those because we have acted rightly. We are what we repeatedly do. Excellence, then, is not an act but a habit.

—Aristotle

[IF I ONLY KNEW THEN WHAT I KNOW NOW™]

LESSON 26

YOU CAN ALWAYS DO THINGS MUCH BETTER AND FASTER THAN YOU THINK YOU CAN

If we were to do all that we are capable of doing, we would literally astonish ourselves.

—Thomas A. Edison

We're experts at putting limits on our dreams and abilities. People will state their limitations without your even asking. But, ask them to tell you their potential and possibilities and see how painstaking the experience becomes for them.

Maybe you're one of them.

If so, why have you let the limiting and constricting beliefs of family, friends and society hold you down?

And why is it that you've concentrated so much on what you *can't* do and not on everything you *can* do?

The truth is, your potential is unlimited. That's right, without *any* limits. And if that's the case, which it is, then why haven't you allowed yourself to do the things you truly desire?

THE LESSON TO BE LEARNED IS...

Think back to a time when you were really challenged to get a job done—a job that seemed nearly impossible—and you did it beyond your own and others' expectations. You pushed yourself out of the rut known as the comfort zone, and you achieved more than you ever thought possible.

Made you feel incredible, didn't it?

You can have that same kind experience every day, in every area of your life, if you will only push yourself just a little bit more.

Your body is the most incredible machine ever designed, and it begs to be worked out—physically, mentally and spiritually—every single day.

Keep pushing it past what it's used to and, amazingly, it always responds by growing, getting stronger and developing greater capacity to learn, remember and do.

Each time you push and expect more from yourself than you're used to, your body and mind respond beautifully and give you that which you want them to.

Always know that your capacity and ability to experience and do better things, greater things, is unlimited.

You have so much awesome power inside you right now.

All you've got to do is use it.

LESSON 27

THE BEST WAY TO LEARN ANYTHING IS BY DOING

*O Lord, thou givest us everything,
at the price of an effort.*
—Leonardo da Vinci

Bookstores are filled with books on virtually any subject you can think of. Whatever it is you want to do, you can find a book on it somewhere.

And while books, magazines, television shows and seminars can give you a lot of good information about whatever you're interested in, the only way you will ever learn it is by doing it.

The world is filled with people who suffer from analysis paralysis. They study, study, study. They learn facts, figures and formulas. Write out elaborate game plans. Buy all the equipment and supplies they'll need, yet barely, if at all, get started. Or if they do, it's a half-baked attempt that usually brings half-baked results.

THE LESSON TO BE LEARNED IS...

If you've never played a musical instrument and someone asks you if you can, don't you dare say no. The truth is, you don't know because you've never tried. Always remember that experience has nothing to do with ability.

You may not have had the experience of painting, speaking or playing a musical instrument, but that has nothing to do with your ability to do those or anything else.

[IF I ONLY KNEW THEN WHAT I KNOW NOW™]

The only way you will ever know is if you try.

The old story of the man who was asked the best way to get to Carnegie Hall and he replied "Practice," is so true.

Just know that it's totally okay to not be the best and to do something poorly when you first start out.

You'll only be a beginner once.

LESSON 28

I WISH I HAD WHAT YOU HAVE

The frustrating thing about life is our neighbors keep buying things we can't afford.
—Anonymous

Amazing isn't it, that so many times we think how much better our lives would be if only we had what others have. Our problems seem so big compared to other folks'. Truly, comparison is one of the biggest reasons for unhappiness.

It's a strange quirk of human nature that people crave those things they don't have and detest the things they're stuck with.

THE LESSON TO BE LEARNED IS...

If you put all your problems in a big pile and you saw everyone else's, chances are you'd take yours back in a heartbeat.

That great spouse the other person has, whom you may secretly wish you could find someone like, may not be that great at all—at least, not for you and what you need.

When you compare your job, your relationships, your car, clothes, home, money and experiences to someone else's, you are setting yourself up for a major feel-bad session.

What works for others, works for others and not necessarily for you; so how can you compare what you need to what they have?

Only you know what it is that makes you happy, and you don't need the approval of anyone else in order to allow yourself to have it or experience it. How can anyone accurately tell you exactly what you need, when they haven't the slightest clue about those things that really make you tick inside?

No one can.

Not your mother, father, spouse, best friend or anyone else.

Only you know what's best for you.

It's time to stop the dead-end, feel-bad comparisons.

Give yourself the relationship, experiences, dreams, goals and things that will bring you the happiness that only you can experience.

LESSON 29

THE SACREDNESS OF FEELINGS

Men are disturbed not by the things that happen,
but by their opinion of the things that happen.
—Epictetus

Many believe that feelings and emotions are what make us human. But do those feelings and emotions make us miserable?

Lots of people place a heavy emphasis on their feelings, with some of them, to the point where those emotions rule their lives.

Yet, they keep forgetting the undeniable fact that they are the only ones who have complete control over their feelings.

You see, you can have any experience or feel any way you want to at any time. That's only your choice. It's how you *perceive* things and what feelings you *choose* to attach to any experience that makes you feel either good or bad, either happy or sad.

THE LESSON TO BE LEARNED IS…

The more sacredness you attach to feelings, the greater you fear that someone, somewhere, sometime may hurt them.

That means that fear factor is always there, controlling how much you'll allow yourself to experience and enjoy in any relationship. You can never truly be free to be yourself, because you're always holding something back.

And because of that, many potentially fabulous friendships, relationships and experiences have had their fires put out too quickly.

But that was then and this is now.

Embrace your feelings as feedback signals that want you to ask questions of yourself, as to why you may feel the way you do about the people, places and events.

The answers you get will give you the insight you need to heal that which has hurt you. And with that insight will come the power you need to propel you to that which you desire.

LESSON 30

THE MAGNET OF ATTRACTION

*Men do not attract that which they want,
but that which they are.*

—James Allen

It's been said that we attract those people in our lives whose ideas and beliefs are similar to our own.

How true.

Still, many people wonder why they always seem to find themselves in unpleasant relationships and business dealings, while they're totally convinced they couldn't possibly attract those kinds of people and problems.

Let's look at a few of these kinds of people.

I call them the drainers, and if you're not careful, they'll suck the life right out of you emotionally, spiritually, physically and financially.

THE LESSON TO BE LEARNED IS...

THE PUMP-ME-UPPERS

These are the people who constantly need to be coached. Seems they are down more than they are up. They tend to focus more on problems than solutions. Their conversation tends to be about events of the past, rather than dreams of the future.

THE LOOKERS

Outwardly, these are some of the most beautiful people around. However, inwardly it's a whole different story.

The old saying, "Pretty is as pretty does," is so true. These folks are really into their appearance to a degree that it becomes an obsession as to what clothes they wear, what car they drive, what job they have, what house they live in and what kind of lucky recipient gets to be in a relationship with them.

THE EXPECTORS

You can never do enough for these people. Not only do they expect you to be there for them emotionally and physically whenever they want, but when you're not, they become upset and blame you for being selfish.

THE ABUSERS

Guilt and physical abuse are the two biggies for these people. They're masters at making you feel like dirt, turning their problems into yours, and playing with your emotions and life like you're a puppet on a string. They should also be called the withholders, because whatever relationship they're in is on their time schedule and on their terms.

THE UNCOMMUNICATORS

These folks want you to feel sorry for them. They pretend like they can't open up, but the reality is that in more situations than not, they've found that keeping quiet about their feelings causes others to feel doubt about themselves and the relationship and actually serves to pull their partner closer. Seems that not knowing how the other feels causes many people to try doubly hard to break the ice and try to help their unemotional partner over their perceived "temporary problem."

THE NEGLECTORS

These are the people who love when you do things for them. Yet, when it comes time for you to receive love and affection back, they give only a little, if at all. Their primary motivation and concern is how you can make them feel good. And, wouldn't you know it, it's never quite the right time for them to talk to you and hug you the way you need those things. Yet, many keep giving to the neglectors in the hopes that one day, the neglector will finally pay them back with interest. That someday never seems to come.

THE FIXERS

These folks need you, and that makes you feel great. The problem is, they need you to fix their problems and help them get their life in order. Many of these people grew up in families where they never had a good role model for relationships. Most of their growing years were in families whose major focus was dealing with issues and problems, to the exclusion of building positive, loving, accepting and unconditional relationships.

What many of these fixers do is find someone with a clean slate (the person with a well-balanced and happy life), then write their problems all over the other person's clean slate. The one with the clean slate is left frustrated and confused, because to them the relationship is unhealthy, unhappy and unfulfilling. After all, sure, there will always be problems we must deal with, but dealing with those problems all the time and making that the focus of the relationship? There's got to be something better.

Yet, to the fixer, unless there are problems and issues in the relationship to always talk about and deal with, the relationship just doesn't feel right and something's wrong. So the fixer pulls away physically, emotionally and spiritually, until the partner with the clean slate decides enough is enough and finally ends the relationship.

Not a problem for the fixer. They simply turn on the deceptive charm, make the next person in their life feel needed and wanted and allow the endless cycle to continue.

LESSON 31

TAKE CONTROL

The best way to predict your future is to create it.

Ever notice how many people are masters at learned helplessness? For some strange reason, they believe that their destiny in life is a matter of chance and not of choice. So many of them are caught in the trap of believing that most of their lives should be spent trying to adjust to circumstances that life happens to throw their way, instead of creating their own circumstances they want to experience.

Many of these people are some of the best people you'd ever want to meet. Many have a deep faith and believe that if they'll only wait long enough, God will step in and put their life in order. The problem is, they expect God to do it all. Little do they remember the old biblical admonition, "God helps those who help themselves."

THE LESSON TO BE LEARNED IS…

You begin to help yourself by taking responsibility for your life—every area of it.

If it isn't working the way you want it to, think again… it's working exactly the way you want it to until you change your thoughts and beliefs about the kind of life you want to be living. Until that happens, you're going to keep getting that which you've been experiencing.

If you're in a job or career you don't like but feel you must stay in because you're too old, you're too young, you don't have enough education or experience or the benefits (a.k.a. the golden handcuffs) and money are too good, think again. That misery and emptiness you feel is brought on by your own choosing. Choose to follow your dream and make life pay off on your own terms, and accept nothing less than the best from yourself.

Take control of your finances by paying yourself (saving/investing) 10% of every dollar you make. And do that *before* you pay any bills. Remember, if you can't save anything on your current income, how will you ever do it with your future income? Take control and reduce your debt by transferring your high-interest credit card balances to low interest credit cards. You can save 50% or more. And these are only two ways for you to take immediate financial control of your future.

Take control of your relationships by refusing to accept anyone or anything less than who and what is best for you. Let go of the belief that you feel trapped and don't have the power to let go. Of course you do. You've always had it. You just haven't used it.

If you're unhappy in a relationship and have tried to work it out and truly believe it has no future, then get out. Keep the lesson and throw away the experience, and be patient until that which you do want, happens. Accept nothing but the best for yourself and don't worry, it will happen.

Always remember that your parents, family, friends and loved ones don't have any control over your life unless you give them that power.

Refuse to be like a little puppet or to change your thoughts and beliefs like the wind when someone discourages you or gives you a disapproving look.

:: The Lessons of Life and What They're Trying to Teach You ::

Only you know what's best for you. And you begin to live it, experience it and have it by taking control of every area of your life today.

[IF I ONLY KNEW THEN WHAT I KNOW NOW™]

LESSON 32

DON'T DOUBT WHAT YOU DON'T HEAR

*Our doubts are traitors and make us lose the good
we oft might win by fearing to attempt.*
—William Shakespeare

One of the strangest things about people is that they doubt what they don't hear.

For example, you've met someone you really care about, and days go by before you receive a call from them. During that time, your mind wanders all over the place, and you start asking yourself all kinds of questions.

Did the other person think as much of me as I of them?

Did I say the right things or did I scare them off?

We'll probably never see each other again, since I haven't heard from them by now.

The same thing happens in business.

You meet with other business people and a deal is made. The other party says they'll call, text or email you by a certain date, yet the calls, texts and emails never come.

So you wonder and doubt about the deal and your ability to make things happen.

THE LESSON TO BE LEARNED IS…

As much as we'd like, people don't operate on our time schedule.

Sure, it would be great to get the call, have the meeting, receive the money, sell the project, get the raise, experience new things when people tell us we will. But many times it doesn't happen like we want. Left unchecked, the "not hearing and doubting" syndrome can play some wild tricks on us.

The one thing your mind loves to do is run free and quickly think of the worst possible outcome, because that's what it's been programmed to do all these years.

Family, friends, loved ones, co-workers and society in general have embraced the belief that it's easier to think of the worst than expect the best. Not hearing from people *when you think you should* only fuels that belief.

Learn to adjust your expectations more in line with other people's time schedules.

Each of us has a different timeframe we feel good about working within. Your goal is to quickly observe the other's timeframe and set your plans and need for answers within it.

By all means, expect the very best in each experience you have every day, but not to the point where anyone has to answer you in a certain way by a certain time.

Go with the flow, and your life will be far less stressful and much more enjoyable.

| LIFE'S WORDS OF WISDOM |

He who is silent is forgotten;
he who abstains is taken at his word;
he who does not advance falls back;
he who stops is overwhelmed,
distanced, crushed;
he who ceases to grow greater
becomes smaller;
he who leaves off, gives up;
the stationary condition
is the beginning of the end.

—Henri Frederic Amiel

[IF I ONLY KNEW THEN WHAT I KNOW NOW™]

LESSON 33

HOLD YOURSELF TO A HIGHER STANDARD

Why have you settled for so little when you can have so much?

Why do people expect so little of themselves?

Their words are a big tip-off.

Many people use lazy language; the same words and phrases over and over without even a thought as to how they sound and the picture of themselves they are painting to others who hear them.

Then there is their daily routine.

They get up at the same time, do the same routine at their job, eat the same kind of food at lunch, come home, eat the same kinds of food at dinner, talk about the same kinds of subjects, watch the same television shows and go to bed at the same time, just to do it all over again tomorrow.

Exciting, huh?

These people are operating at just slightly above the required expenditure to stay alive. If they were a 400-horsepower engine, they'd be using about 25 horsepower and then they complain that they're always tired or don't have enough time to do that which they really don't want to but say they do.

THE LESSON TO BE LEARNED IS…

One of the biggest reasons your life, the way you look, the people you associate with and the things you experience are the way they are is because of what you have allowed yourself to accept. They simply represent a certain standard you think things should meet, and everything you do or allow yourself to experience must fit within your predetermined standard.

The great news is you can change any or all of them by picturing yourself as someone different than you are right now and by seeing yourself as someone you'd really like to be.

Freedom is knowing that all those unpleasant and unhappy and unfulfilling things you may be tolerating right now, or have tolerated in the past, can be changed once you set a higher standard for yourself.

See yourself as someone incredibly talented and uniquely gifted, someone who won't settle for anything but the best.

Accept nothing less, because you're capable of more.

And understand this inescapable fact: *People will treat you the way you train them to treat you. And the way you train them to treat you is by setting the standard of treatment you believe you deserve.*

:: The Lessons of Life and What They're Trying to Teach You ::

LESSON 34

YOUR LIFE IS EXCITING IN PROPORTION TO THE NUMBER OF THINGS YOU HAVE TO LOOK FORWARD TO

Life is a series of surprises, and would not be worth taking or keeping if it were not.
—Ralph Waldo Emerson

Think about how happy you are when you have something to look forward to.

A vacation, moving into a new home or getting a new car, meeting someone, a new job, eating at a new restaurant or seeing a new movie—they all add to the excitement of your life, because you are looking forward to them.

Of course, being involved in lots of projects keeps your life exciting, but that's only part of it. The number of things you have to look forward to is directly related to how often, and to what degree, you break out of the comfort zone.

I'm amazed at the number of people who complain about their boring lives, yet do little or nothing to change things.

When asked how many times they go out to dinner, they say maybe once or twice a month and it's usually to the same places, when there are countless restaurant experiences just waiting to be had. All they'd need to do is get in the car and walk through the door and—voila!—a new experience.

Boring people lead boring lives.

If you're one of them, the only way to change that is to break out of the comfort zone and expand your possibilities for experience.

THE LESSON TO BE LEARNED IS…

The comfort zone can be one of the fastest ways for you to wither and die. Not only will it keep you doing the things you've been doing and forcing you to accept the same things you've been accepting, but it will always seek to keep you there.

Not only that, the comfort zone will continually seek to lower your expectations even further—giving you the ideas, attitudes and beliefs to support why you think you should not experience new things—thereby continually reducing those things you have to look forward to.

Understand that when you look forward to things, you're thinking *future;* and when you think *future*, you tend to be positive.

The more you have to look forward to, the more you think *future*, the more you give your mind a target to shoot for and the more positive your mind will stay.

Now that's exciting!

LESSON 35

PEOPLE ARE A LOT LIKE ANIMALS: WITH HURT OR PAIN COMES A DEEP NEED TO BE LEFT ALONE

Unless a man takes himself sometimes out of the world, by retirement and self-reflection, he will be in danger of losing himself in the world.
—Benjamin Whichcote

As much as society tells us that we need a support team of friends, family and loved ones, the undeniable truth is that when it comes to hurt or pain, we have a deep need to be left alone.

It's in these times of hurt and pain that we realize so much about ourselves, who we are, where we've been, why we're at this point in our lives and where we'd most like to go. Even with the greatest love and intentions, no one can give us the answers to those questions.

Hurt and pain also reveal to us, if we only open our hearts and eyes, that an incredible life force within us guides us unerringly and perfectly to exactly where we need to be at that exact time in our life.

No book, lecture, tape, seminar or expert can do that.

Nor should we depend on them to. For it is within every single one of us that we have the power to come back from any hurt or pain and be stronger and wiser as a result of it.

THE LESSON TO BE LEARNED IS…

Give yourself time to be alone to hear that still, small voice within that calls you to stop, slow down, heal and reflect on the important lessons you may have been neglecting.

Those lessons will keep coming back in your life, over and over, until you learn from them.

Being alone during this time will also show you how important it is to take time to be by yourself on a daily basis—even if only for a few minutes each day, and even when you're not hurting or going through pain. In fact, that's one of the best ways to keep you from going through so much of it on the first place.

[IF I ONLY KNEW THEN WHAT I KNOW NOW™]

LESSON 36

NO ONE CAN MAKE YOU UPSET WITHOUT YOUR PERMISSION

I envy the beasts two things—their ignorance of evil to come, and their ignorance of what is said about them.

—Voltaire

For some, getting upset is like a full-time job. Seems there's never a shortage of people and things to get upset about.

For many, it doesn't stop there.

They not only get upset easily, but they love telling people about what someone did to upset them. Along with that, they have this uncanny ability to relive every minute detail until the imagined hurt becomes greater than what happened in real life.

Yet, ask these people to describe—with the same vivid detail and myriad emotions—their big dreams for their life, and they'll look at you in confusion and then become upset at you for asking, because they've never taken the time to think about something so unimportant.

THE LESSON TO BE LEARNED IS...

No one can make you upset unless you first give them permission to do so. You are the only one who has that power, and you give your power away to the other person when you allow them to control your feelings and happiness.

You see, whatever happens to you is neutral; it's neither good nor bad. It's your perception of it, and putting your own label on it that makes you feel good or unhappy.

But it is only you who can apply that label.

If a friend stood next to you and watched an event or listened to words being spoken by someone you knew, you both would have two very different perceptions of what really happened.

To you, that action or those words spoken may upset you. To your friend, who doesn't have all your past experiences and conditioning, all those things you both witnessed together were just neutral events that happened with no emotion attached to either one.

Yet, when you make yourself feel good or bad is when you let your mind put on it whatever label it wants to, without first asking yourself, "Why is it important for me to label this?"

What you're going to find is that by consciously taking control over your mind and your thoughts, you can choose to look at everything that happens to you as a positive learning experience that will only help you move closer to becoming the person you truly want to be.

And you'll always remember that no one, at any time or anywhere, can ever make you upset without your permission.

LIFE'S WORDS OF WISDOM

It is not the critic who counts; not the man who points out how the strong man stumbles, or where the doer of deeds could have done them better. The credit belongs to the man who is actually in the arena, whose face is marred by dust and sweat and blood, who strives valiantly; who errs and comes short again and again; because there is not effort without error and shortcomings; but who does actually strive to do the deed; who knows the great enthusiasm, the great devotion, who spends himself in a worthy cause, who at the best knows in the end the triumph of high achievement and who at the worst, if he fails, at least he fails while daring greatly. So that his place shall never be with those cold and timid souls who know neither victory nor defeat.

—Theodore Roosevelt

[IF I ONLY KNEW THEN WHAT I KNOW NOW™]

LESSON 37

PEOPLE LOVE THE UNDERDOG

Adversity causes some men to break: others to break records.
—William A. Ward

Ever see two teams playing each other and the defending champions are viewed as this group of cocky, uppity players who keep winning all the time? So who is it that most people want to win? The underdogs.

That's the way life is.

People love the Comeback Kid and the hero who beat all odds to win.

They love them because these people represent all that's good about the human spirit. A spirit that knows nothing of defeat and one that can defy all odds to make the seemingly impossible, possible.

That's exactly the same kind of spirit you need to be the great success you can be.

THE LESSON TO BE LEARNED IS…

Imagine yourself in a world where there are so many cutthroat people who would love to use you to help them get to where they want to be.

Imagine these people climbing to the top, but as they do so, they lie, steal and hurt others along the way.

Just imagine these are the same people who may have told you that you don't have what it takes to make it and you might as well go home and forget your dreams.

:: The Lessons of Life and What They're Trying to Teach You ::

But you don't listen.

Deep within you are incredible talents and abilities that others have no idea about.

So, as these users enjoy their temporary ride to the top, you retain all the ethics and qualities these others wouldn't: hard work, commitment, focus, humility, honesty, integrity, honor, trust, bridge building of solid friendships, service to others and doing everything else that will make you the very best you are capable of.

And quietly, under the radar, you begin to rise.

At first, what you do isn't even noticed.

Then, as you keep climbing and going for your dreams, something phenomenal begins to happen.

You begin sensing that others are getting behind you and want to see you make it to the top. Even those who you never thought would be there for you are there now, cheering you on in their own special way.

To them, you've always been the underdog.

Your unpretentious and caring positive attitude only makes them want to see you win, and win big.

Always think of yourself as a champion who is the underdog, and you'll have more friends than you can imagine there to support you as you continually enjoy all the blessings of being a true winner.

[IF I ONLY KNEW THEN WHAT I KNOW NOW™]

LESSON 38

NEVER DO ANYTHING YOU CAN PAY SOMEONE ELSE TO DO BETTER THAN YOU

Man is here for the sake of other men.
—Albert Einstein

Many years ago, the late wealthy industrialist Andrew Carnegie told that to *Think And Grow Rich* author Napoleon Hill, and the admonition surprised him. Yet the more he thought about it, the more it made perfect sense.

You and everyone else on this planet have the same 24 hours in a day. You also have a limited amount of time—called your life—that you can use any way you choose. You no doubt have lots of things you want to do that are important to you. Yet, washing your car, painting your house and cleaning your carpets or your house are only a few of the things that use your precious time and don't leave any for the things you truly want to do.

THE LESSON TO BE LEARNED IS...

How much is your time worth?

Seriously, I want you to tell me: How valuable is your time?

Are you worth $20 dollars an hour? $50? $100? More? I want you to put a price on your time and you'll soon see why.

Let's say your time is worth $50 dollars an hour to you.

:: The Lessons of Life and What They're Trying to Teach You ::

So you decide to wash your car. You get out the hoses, bucket, soap, washrags, chamois, glass cleaner, rubber preservative and vacuum, and you go to town.

An hour later, you're just about finished when you realize you could have taken the car to a car wash, paid $14.95, saved $35.00 of your time and would've been finished much sooner.

The smart thing to do—unless of course, you absolutely love doing these things—is to leave the all the jobs you're not an expert at, to those who are. You're not only saving time and money, you're also creating income and opportunities for other people.

Now that's a great feeling.

Give up the need for perfection or the need to do everything yourself.

You simply don't have the time to be losing so much of your money.

LESSON 39

RICH IS THE PERSON WHO MAKES THEIR INCOME FIT THE LIFESTYLE. POOR IS THE PERSON WHO MAKES THEIR LIFESTYLE FIT THEIR INCOME.

Being broke is only temporary; being poor is a state of mind.
—Anonymous

So let's talk more money.

It's amazing how many people live within their means instead of creating more means for which they can live.

It's too bad that far too many people live by the belief that "money talks, but mine only knows how to say 'good-bye.'"

But can you really blame them?

We come by our beliefs honestly, now, don't we?

Chances are our parents, their parents, their friends and family all grew up with the belief that success in life means putting in more hours at a job that's unfulfilling but steady.

Work that overtime, hope for a cost of living raise and maybe a nice bonus at the holidays and those things can change their lives.

It rarely does.

THE LESSON TO BE LEARNED IS…

The thing I keep pounding home is that your income in life is dependent on one thing: your service to others.

:: The Lessons of Life and What They're Trying to Teach You ::

Increase your service to others and you get more rewards. Yes, more money and opportunity.

If you waited for your job to give you the kind of life you want, chances are it's never going to happen.

Health and fitness legend Joe Weider always told me, "You'll never get rich working for someone else." This comes from a guy who started his worldwide health and fitness empire with only $7 in a small room in his parents' home, and built it into a worldwide fitness movement worth billions of dollars.

Joe is absolutely right.

Be your own boss.

The backbone of America is small businesses. And in more than 100 years, this fact has not changed.

Right now, there is something you can do better than anyone else out there. Something that can bring you all the wealth, success, happiness and deep inner fulfillment and meaning you want, if only you will follow your dream and do what you've always wanted to do.

By doing so, you will quickly learn that whenever you want to give yourself a raise, you can do it simply by providing your service to more and more people.

Remember: More service = more rewards, which means more money.

Soon you'll be having what you want instead of wanting something different from what you already have.

LESSON 40

DO THE THINGS THAT ADD TO YOUR HAPPINESS

*The way to happiness:
keep your heart free from hate, your mind
free from worry. Live simply, expect little,
give much. Fill your life with love. Scatter sunshine.
Forget self, think of others. Do as you would be done by.
Try this for a week and you will be surprised.*
—H.C. Mattern

Life is much too short to be doing anything that takes away from your happiness.

Why is it that people feel this perverse sense of duty to get into relationships, jobs and situations in life that totally drain them of creativity, spontaneity, joy, accomplishment, fulfillment and happiness? It's almost as if they feel that they'll be rewarded at the end of their life if only they can go through enough crap and heartache while they're living now.

THE LESSON TO BE LEARNED IS...

Just so you'll know, the only time you have is now to make yourself and give yourself the things and experiences that will bring you happiness.

I've yet to hear from anyone who has passed from this earth who has come back and said, "Tell everyone that their reward in heaven is in direct proportion to how much of a miserable life they live on this earth."

Unless you heard that message from someone on the other side, then don't believe it.

Surround yourself with the people who bring you joy and encouragement, those who are positive and fill you with the belief that great things can and will happen for you. Accept nothing less, because you don't have to.

Simply ask yourself: Do the people and experiences in your life add to your happiness?

If the answer is yes, keep them.

If the answer is no, look at why; and if you're having problems coming up with good reasons, then it's time to make a change. And there's no better time than now.

LESSON 41

THE BRAIN DRAIN

If you deliberately plan to be less than you are capable of being, then I warn you, that you will be unhappy for the rest of your life. You will be evading your own capacities and possibilities.

—Dr. Abraham Maslow

Your mind is like a high-performance Ferrari.

You can drive the Ferrari around town at 30 to 40 miles per hour and it will get you to where you want to go. Yet, the Ferrari is built for speed. It's designed to go fast, and it can do it for long periods without needing a rest.

That's the way your mind is, too.

You see, when you allow yourself to settle in on a job, your mind will find the comfort level where it can do the required amount of work with the minimal amount of effort. And because you accept this comfort level, you never really grow and expand.

But that's not the way the bigger part of you wants it to be.

THE LESSON TO BE LEARNED IS...

Inside you is always that still small voice, urging you to grow, to learn and to become more than you are right now. Your mind keeps playing these messages to you in the hopes that you'll listen and follow its leading.

What happens is that when you don't listen to these important messages, tension is created inside you because

:: The Lessons of Life and What They're Trying to Teach You ::

of where you are right now and where your mind knows you can and need to be.

Because the mind seeks to keep harmony and balance inside you, these messages calling you to change keep playing, but they get fainter and fainter until finally, all that's left is a dull ache inside you that keeps pulling on your heartstrings until you follow its calling.

And until you follow its calling, the mind throttles down and operates well below what you're capable of, just to keep some sense of balance until you're sick and tired of not changing and growing.

Yet as soon as you signal that you want to change and you want something different, something better, your minds starts that Ferrari engine inside you and is fueled up and ready to take you where it knows best, where you should go.

It's time for you to enjoy the ride.

LIFE'S WORDS OF WISDOM

Never build a case against yourself.

—Robert Rowbottom

LESSON 42

BE YOUR OWN BEST FRIEND

I am somebody. I am me. I like being me.
And I need nobody to make me somebody.
—Louis L'Amour

Many people spend their entire lives in search of validation and acceptance and becoming everyone else's best friend except their own.

The need to feel important, wanted, needed and appreciated is so deep a human craving that many people give up the essence of who they are to find it.

They rarely succeed in that quest.

THE LESSON TO BE LEARNED IS...

The only person you can depend on is you.

Understand that everything that has happened, is happening or will happen to you is the direct result of what you allowed, are allowing, or will allow to happen.

You are the only one who will allow yourself to have whatever you believe you are worthy of experiencing.

If you see yourself as a loser, then you'll surround yourself with people just like you who expect little out of life and are rarely disappointed.

However, if you see yourself as your own best friend, the one who's been there for you ever since you were born, and who will always be there for you and accepts you totally and unconditionally, you will find a sense of inner peace and happiness others can only wish for.

Think of how you would want a best friend to treat you.

They would believe in you.

They would trust in you.

They would accept you for who you are and what you are at any and all times.

They would encourage you and make you feel great about yourself.

They wouldn't care how much or how little money or material things you had.

All they would care about is you.

That's a true friend. That's a best friend. That's the kind of friend who's inside you right now.

Allow that friend to come out. After all, that friend is going to be with you for the rest of your life.

| LIFE'S WORDS OF WISDOM |

You experience in your life whatever it is you're deeply convinced is true. If much of your thinking is about what you don't have, who you're not, what you can't have, and that you're a bad person, you'll continue to create the conditions in your life that make those thoughts come true.

LESSON 43

KEEP YOUR MIND ON THE THINGS YOU WANT AND OFF THE THINGS YOU DON'T WANT

The thing always happens that you really believe in; and the belief in a thing makes it happen.

—Frank Lloyd Wright

Sounds so easy. So why is it so hard?

Perhaps it's because people don't realize the real truth behind that statement.

THE LESSON TO BE LEARNED IS...

Keeping your mind focused on what you don't want only attracts and brings to you more of that which you don't want.

Your mind is like a magnet. The dominating thoughts you think send out incredibly powerful messages that bring into your life everything related to your dominant thoughts.

After all, by thinking these things all the time, you're only telling your mind exactly what it is that you want to keep on experiencing. Your mind's job is to follow your commands, and it does so with absolutely incredible reliability.

The quickest and most powerful way to change what you have in your life is to focus only on that which you want.

Doing so gives your mind a new and different target to aim for, and a new goal to achieve.

Just like it once brought more of that which you don't want, it will now bring everything you do want.

And who said this thing called "changing your life for the better" wasn't any fun!

| LIFE'S WORDS OF WISDOM |

Sow a thought and you reap an Act:
Sow an Act, and you reap a Habit;
Sow a Habit, and you reap a Character;
Sow a Character, and you reap a Destiny.

—Samuel Smiles

LESSON 44

YOU WERE GIVEN COMPLETE UNCHALLENGEABLE CONTROL OVER JUST ONE THING, AND IT'S CALLED "YOUR THOUGHTS"

Nurture great thoughts for you will never go higher than your thoughts.

—Anonymous

It's been said that of all the things the Creator could have given you complete and unchallengeable control over, It gave only one: the power of your thoughts.

Yes, other people, the government and your company can do a lot of things that you have no control over. Yet, what no one ever can or will be able to take away from you are the thoughts you think and the dreams you dream.

No one.

THE LESSON TO BE LEARNED IS...

If thoughts are so important, what does that mean to you?

Well, your dominant thoughts do actually clothe themselves in their physical reality. Thoughts become physical things: What you think about, you bring about.

Of course, you can't think about a new car and have it suddenly appear. It doesn't quite work like that. However, how it does work is that if you vividly imagine yourself having a certain kind of car, visualize that car sitting in your garage, feel yourself in the seat of that car and enjoying the thrill of driving it, soon your mind will present ways to you of how you can have that car. Ways you probably never even dreamed of.

You see, your mind doesn't know the difference between a real experience or an imagined one.

The mind's only job is to bring into your life all those things that relate to your dominant thoughts. How your mind does that is beyond our finding out. The most important thing is it doesn't matter how it does it. Just be absolutely assured it does and it never fails. Never.

But for your mind to do that, you must first direct your thoughts on only those things you want.

Stay completely focused on them.

Believe with all your heart that you have them and are enjoying them right now. For the more vivid the picture of what you want and the more emotion you put into it, the faster your mind will bring whatever you want into your life.

LIFE'S WORDS OF WISDOM

Faith is the force of life.

—Leo Tolstoy

LESSON 45

THOSE WITH BIG FAITH GET BIG RESULTS

It is the young man of little faith who says, 'I am nothing.'
It is the young man of true conception who says,
'I am everything' and then goes to prove it.
—Edward W. Bok

Just as no one can see your thoughts, the same is true for your faith. Only your actions reveal to everyone what it is you truly believe.

The problem many people have is that they have faith but they must first see it before they believe it.

That's not faith, that's doubt. For faith truly is the assurance of things hoped for and the conviction of things not yet seen.

History is filled with great people who faced incredible adversity, hardship and pain, only to have lost everything but their faith. And faith was the very thing that carried them through any and every difficulty and made them come out a winner.

THE LESSON TO BE LEARNED IS...

Faith is actually belief that the unseen will happen.

Let me give you a real life example. I had the opportunity to meet former world heavyweight boxing champion Evander Holyfield at his home one day. His training partner was eight-time Mr. Olympia bodybuilding champion, Lee Haney.

Now, Lee is a very spiritual man, someone you just love to be around because his faith and belief in God send so much positive energy out to everyone he meets that it's contagious, whether you're a believer or not.

As I watched Lee and Evander train, I was struck by this incredible power that each great man possessed.

They had faith and lots of it.

At the time, people and the press had written Evander off as having heart problems and being past his prime. Yet, Evander knew differently. His faith never allowed him to accept what others said.

Only be months after my visit he pulled off one of the greatest upsets in boxing history by beating Mike Tyson and at that time becoming only the second man ever, besides Muhammad Ali, to win the heavyweight crown three times.

But Evander told everyone he would do it way before the fight. They looked at him like he was crazy. And when he did win, everyone was surprised but Evander.

He and Lee lived by the creed that big faith gets big results and little faith gets little results.

So I ask you, what kind of faith and what kind of results do you want for your life?

I have big faith in you that you know the answer.

LESSON 46

THE ONE-UPPERS

It is in the character of very few men to honor without envy a friend who has prospered.
—Aeschylus

Tell me if this doesn't sound familiar.

You just had an incredible experience or some great news that you can't wait to tell your friends about. I mean you've been waiting for this news for a long time and now, it's finally happened even better than you thought it would.

So you tell everyone and as soon as you're finished, the one-upper steps in to do their job, "Well, if you think that's good, you should hear what happened to me...."

Poof! Out goes the air in your happiness balloon.

THE LESSON TO BE LEARNED IS...

The world is filled with these kinds of people and they can't stand to see someone happier, more fulfilled or more successful than they are. They can be some of the nicest people you'll ever meet, but along with that kindness comes their tendency to one-up you every chance they get.

Their goal is to not only feel superior by minimizing your experiences but also keep you down by making it uncomfortable for you to want to share any other good news in the future. As a result, you feel frustrated and empty.

:: The Lessons of Life and What They're Trying to Teach You ::

So what can you do?

The best thing is to let go of the one-uppers and send them off and out of your life.

They may be your only friends right now, but that won't be for long. Getting rid of their condescending attitude will be like getting rid of a heavy anchor that's been weighing you down for too long.

With excess baggage gone, you can now be yourself and meet the kind of people you want to know about and those who *want* you to tell them all the great news of your life.

[IF I ONLY KNEW THEN WHAT I KNOW NOW™]

LESSON 47

YOU ARE A MIND WITH A BODY

Take care of the inside and the outside will take care of itself.

An old sage once said, "Your body was designed to carry your mind. Not the only way around."

Here's a little something else for you to ponder: Your body can't think; it only responds to the commands given to it by your mind.

Does your body tell your mind when to breathe?

No.

Does your body tell your mind when and how to heal a cut? No.

Your mind is the command center for anything and everything that happens to your body.

Yet most people still believe that fixing the outside first will change the inside.

Sorry, it doesn't work that way.

THE LESSON TO BE LEARNED IS...

Look at the way you look.

You have the body you now have because that's exactly the body you believe you should have. It fits your picture of the body and performance level you've accepted for yourself to have. And it can be no different until you first change the picture in your mind (inside) of how your body should look and feel.

:: The Lessons of Life and What They're Trying to Teach You ::

For many people that's an uncomfortable thought.

Why on earth would you choose to look like this when for so long you've told everyone and even yourself that you want to look and feel better?

Again, give your mind a new picture to work on and it will show you how you can achieve it.

Any kind of long-term and lasting change must first come from the inside. See and believe yourself as a smarter, more energetic and healthier, and a dynamic, enthusiastic and incredibly blessed and successful person, and you will become that person in a very short time.

But first, change the inside.

The outside will take care of itself.

LESSON 48

REVEAL WHAT YOU WILL FOR THE ANSWER YOU WANT

Men willingly believe what they wish.
—Julius Caesar

Many times in life, we ask people for advice about matters important to us, and when we don't get the answers we're looking for, we get frustrated. We can easily come to the conclusion that others are uncaring and really don't value us. The trouble is, much of the problem could be our fault.

THE LESSON TO BE LEARNED IS…

People can and will only give you advice based on the information you reveal to them and the experiences and frames of references they have had in their lives. No one except you knows the answer for what you need to do at any given time for anything in your life.

The more information you give to others, the better the answer you will get from them. By selectively leaving out information that could be important in helping others understand your problem, you only fuel the fire of frustration, because no one can be a mind reader for you.

Understand that even with giving your loved ones and closest friends so much information, they will never be able to fully relate to you, because they weren't always there to experience all you experienced or saw or heard, the way you did.

:: The Lessons of Life and What They're Trying to Teach You ::

While others may give you feedback as to whether you're on the right course, you're the only one who knows the destinations you ultimately seek and how best to get there.

[IF I ONLY KNEW THEN WHAT I KNOW NOW™]

LESSON 49

YOU DON'T HAVE TO BE ANYTHING EXCEPT YOURSELF

This above all: to thine own self be true;
And it must follow; as the night follows the day, thou then canst not be false to any man.
—William Shakespeare

Yes, the world is full of people who love playing the roles of actors and actresses, yet never revealing their true personality for the world to see.

Such a shame, for when you *try* to make an impression, that's exactly the kind of impression you make—that you're acting.

Why is it so many feel the need to abandon themselves and put on the uncomfortable facade of thinking they're fitting into the role that everyone wants them to be?

THE LESSON TO BE LEARNED IS…

Of all the billions of people on this earth, only you have your own kind of personality.

No one else before, right now, or after you leave this earth will ever have the unique and once-in-a-lifetime traits that make up your personality.

No one.

So why on earth would you ever want to be something you're not?

Perhaps even more enlightening is this: Why would you or anyone try to change someone else just so they can become what you want them to be?

There's no need for it except the need to control.

And much of that need for control comes from the fact you are not letting your real personality come out.

When you accept the beauty of your true self, you then accept, without reservation, question or condition, the real personality of everyone around you.

If, as Shakespeare so eloquently put it, all the world is a stage and we are merely players, isn't it time you play the only part you were created for?

You do by revealing only your true personality for the world and everyone to see, and the time to do it is now.

LESSON 50

THINGS JUST ARE

We exaggerate misfortune and happiness alike.
We are never so wretched or so happy as we say we are.
—Honore de Balzac

In life, things and experiences are neither good nor bad; they just are. It's our thinking and need to put a label on whatever we experience that makes them so.

Why can't we just let things be, and not be so judgmental? Seems that everything we see, read, hear, do or experience needs a label put on it so we can feel better (or worse) about its relationship to and importance in our lives.

But does it really need to be that way?

THE LESSON TO BE LEARNED IS...

The truth is, things just are. And for the most part, there's no need to judge them or make a decision on them.

The whole key to understanding what happens to you and your life is just to be open to experiencing all things at all times, and to allow yourself to let everything soak in and let your brain naturally and unhurriedly present a message to you about what it has been experiencing and what direction or decision would be wise for you to make regarding those things.

Forget about forcing an answer so you can feel better about compartmentalizing and putting everything in its place.

You simply don't need to put that much pressure on yourself.

Once you realize that no one except you is making that demand upon yourself, your need to judge everything and everyone will greatly diminish, and your ability to simply enjoy the experience will greatly increase.

Finally, you'll be able to just accept the fact that things just are. And you know what? That's okay.

LESSON 51

THERE'S NOTHING LIKE EXPERIENCING SOMETHING FOR THE FIRST TIME

When people are bored, it is primarily with their own selves that they are bored.
—Eric Hoffer

Think back to some of your first experiences.

The first time you learned to tie your shoes, your first day in school, the first time you drove a car, your first date, your first love. Oh, what magical and life-changing experiences those and so many other things were!

The beauty of experiencing something for the first time is that it will never end.

Never.

Forget about growing older, having a family, staying in the same old dead-end job, or going to same old vacation spot year after year. None of those things can keep you from experiencing the incredible joy of experiencing things for the first time.

THE LESSON TO BE LEARNED...

If it has been a long time since you've experienced something for the first time, it's because you haven't allowed yourself that experience.

Allowing yourself to be stuck in a rut—and of course by now you know that a rut is simply a grave with both ends removed—by doing the same old thing, over and over, day in and day out, makes your life boring and steals your ability and opportunity to experience new and exciting things—perhaps even for the first time.

Think back to how excited you used to be, not too long ago, about what it felt like to anticipate something for the first time.

I'm here to tell you that those same great feelings and so many others you have yet to experience are still within you, just waiting to be released—if only you will let them.

You are the only one who can do it.

It's time to stop blaming anyone else or circumstances for your not experiencing new things for the first time.

Right now, you could go to a new restaurant, a new store, a new area of your town you've never seen and see and do so many other new, first-time things. What a cool little gift to give to yourself!

Your life truly is exciting in proportion to the number of things you have to look forward to.

The great news is that you don't have to look forward to the same old things. You've been there and done that.

It's time to give your life the excitement of something *new*.

LIFE'S WORDS OF WISDOM

If you have tried and met with defeat; if you have planned and watched your plans as they were crushed before your eyes; just remember that the greatest men in all history were the products of courage, and courage, you know, is born in the cradle of adversity.

—Napoleon Hill

[IF I ONLY KNEW THEN WHAT I KNOW NOW™]

LESSON 52

GOING THROUGH HARD TIMES MAKES YOU APPRECIATE THE GOOD TIMES

I would have never amounted to anything were it not for adversity. I was forced to come up the hard way.
—J. C. Penney

In studying the lives of successful people, one conclusion can be drawn with absolute certainty: Each one went through tough times before experiencing the good times.

Perhaps even more remarkable is the fact that the speed and depth of their success was dependent upon how difficult those tough times were.

In other words, the tougher and more painful the times they went through, the more they resolved to get over it and do whatever they needed to do to learn from it and move on.

THE LESSON TO BE LEARNED IS…

When it comes to tough times, our first instinct is to try and avoid them and protect ourselves from any discomfort, pain or hurt.

Yet life doesn't operate that way.

Often, the tough times in your life are caused by your stubbornness to change something in your life that is not happening or working.

It's as if Nature steps in and says, "Well, I've tried to get your attention to change things in your life and go in a different direction, but you won't listen; so you must suffer the consequences of your stubbornness."

The truth is, tough times change you and forge you into something you need to be in order for you to move to your next level of growth.

And those tough times and pain will continue for the rest of your life—albeit in different forms, faces, names and places—until you learn the lessons you're supposed to learn from them.

You see, tough times give you an appreciation for the good times, and by going through the trials, tribulations and fire of life, you embrace and become more sensitive to those things that are not working in your life.

Not only that, but you're now able to change things more quickly and precisely because the pain of tough times has made you grow and become more aware.

Always embrace the tough times, because your life is calling you to change. Take comfort and strength in the fact that what you're going through is something that someone, somewhere, at some time, has also gone through and has come out victorious.

You will too.

LIFE'S WORDS OF WISDOM

"Mr. Getty, what is it that money cannot buy?"

J. Paul Getty replied, "I don't think it can buy health and I don't think it can buy a good time. Some of the best times I have ever had didn't cost me any money."

LESSON 53

TAKE GOOD CARE OF THINGS

Joy is not in things, it is in us.
—Richard Wagner

It can be said that how you take care of things is also a good indicator of how you take care of yourself.

The things you have in life are merely extensions of you; you like the things that make you feel good and you avoid the things that don't.

Taking care of things—within healthy limits—usually gives people a good feeling of accomplishment and appreciation for the blessings in their lives. But for some, that's not always the case.

If you will observe people and their relationships to the things they own and use, you will find many revealing signs.

THE LESSON TO BE LEARNED IS…

Take a look at the following descriptions of people and their things and see where you might fit in.

THE COLLECTOR

Loves to collect things for the sake of collecting. Usually driven by some level of insecurity and fear that what they want is rare and scarce. And having more of the things others want makes them feel secure, wanted, looked up to and appreciated. But the collector can never relax, because there's always something new to collect that could be bigger, better and more valuable. The collector can never have enough.

THE CLEANER

The cleaner is one who's obsessed with keeping things spotless to the exclusion of not wanting to use the object in the fear that it might get dirty or broken. The cleaner feels great while cleaning and even has a great deal of pride after being finished with a job well done. But, that's where the good feelings end. Ultimately, there's frustration because sooner or later, they're bound to use what they don't want to get dirty or broken, and then they've got to clean it all over again. Like the collector, their work is never done.

THE USER

The user is the one who sees things for what they are, takes care of them the best they can for the time they can allow and uses each thing to get more out of life. The user understands that nothing lasts forever and things are never more important than people. They also know that things can be replaced, whereas people, relationships and experiences cannot.

THE ABUSER

In a sense, the abuser is like the user, but can't be bothered and doesn't take care of the things they want and need in their life. Abusers have a bit of a rebel in them and show their true colors by rejecting the accepted norm, "If you take care of things, they will take care of you." In many cases, the abusers' pattern of lack of caring shows up not only in the things they own—which are only for a short time since they break from lack of care or abuse—but in their relationships to people and life as well.

LESSON 54

THE ONLY PRESSURE YOU HAVE IS THAT WHICH YOU PUT ON YOURSELF

The greatest griefs are those we cause ourselves.

—Sophocles

Take a good look at how many people get frustrated and upset because of all the pressure in their lives. Seems that everywhere they turn, someone is making some type of demand for their time, energy, money, love and talents.

THE LESSON TO BE LEARNED IS...

The only pressure you feel is that which you put on yourself.

Sure, we all have deadlines from time to time, but most of the pressures from those deadlines could be easily avoided if only you would make better use of your time. That means being more disciplined, not waiting until the last minute to do an assignment and seeing the "pressure" situation in a different light.

Think back to when you felt pressure. Wasn't much of the pressure you felt because you felt a bit—or maybe a lot—out of control of the situation and your life at that given moment?

Always remember that you are the only one who has complete and unchallengeable control over your thoughts.

:: The Lessons of Life and What They're Trying to Teach You ::

And by directing your thoughts and seeing things, people and situations for what they truly are—instead of what someone tells you or what you've always believed they are—you then take control of your life and finally release the pressure you've been putting on yourself.

LESSON 55

ASSUMPTION IS THE MOTHER OF MANY FOUL-UPS

You believe that easily which you hope for earnestly.
—Publius Terentius Terence

How many times have you assumed somebody would do something or something would happen and it didn't?

I would bet it's a lot.

So why is it that, even after we've been let down and disappointed, we still assume so much from so many so often?

Well, our human nature is such that we want to believe the best in others, but if you're not careful, that can cause problems.

THE LESSON TO BE LEARNED IS...

The problem with assumption is that it's based on the idea that others view our wishes and hopes the same as we do.

That what you desire is what someone else desires just as much as you do, and that others want to make your plans work out in the same way you want them to.

That the timeframe you want something to happen in is the very same timeframe that others will work to make your desires come true.

But we know that people don't always work like that.

In fact, they seldom work like that.

You see, other people have their own agenda and timeframe, even if they want to help you accomplish your goals and dreams. A key to your success and moving things in your life forward is knowing their agenda and timeframe. Doing so will save you days, weeks and months of disappointment and frustration—not to mention substantial amounts of time and money.

Here's the big secret: Assume nothing.

In business, get things in writing so everyone knows what's expected of each other and by what timeframe.

The *only* thing you should assume is that the other person needs to have a comprehensive map, guide and instructions from you as to what you expect of them and when you expect it.

Without that, you would be wise to assume that assumption will continue to be the mother of many foul-ups.

LESSON 56

HOW WELL ARE YOU TRAINED?

Don't believe you're traveling down the right road just because everyone else is too.
—Anonymous

Study human behavior and you begin noticing something very interesting: People are a lot like trained animals.

While many of them don't even realize they've been trained, their daily actions and predictable responses and reactions show just how well they've been trained.

But at what cost is the desire to be well trained keeping you from having the kind of life that awaits you?

THE LESSON TO BE LEARNED IS…

One of the hardest things to do is to break out of the mold of doing the same thing over and over, year after year, without a lot of thought as to why.

That's one way you've trained yourself to accept your lot in life and just go with the flow, whatever that flow may bring you.

But, those darned dreams of yours keep coming up at the times you don't even expect them, and they start you wondering what it would be like to do something new and different. To do the thing you've always wanted to but never have, because of fear.

So you think about it and what your life would be like, and for a moment it feels incredible.

Then you start to feel real uncomfortable.

Quickly you try to forget your dreams and go back to what you've trained yourself to do and feel.

Well, I've got some really good news for you.

Just as you trained yourself to accept misery, frustration, unhappiness and struggle, you can just as easily train yourself to accept the kind of new life that you've really wanted and desired.

The way you do that is by allowing yourself to feel, see and imagine what your life would be like if you were doing the things that you truly wanted to do.

Forget about knowing the right people, having the right contacts or enough money or experience—those things don't make a hill of beans' worth of difference in regards to where you are right now and where you want to go.

Each day, especially at night before you go to bed and in the morning as soon as you awake, let yourself be free to dream, imagine and experience in your mind the changes you want to make in your life.

Remember: Where the mind goes, the body follows; and where your mental images and pictures go—with emotional conviction—your subconscious mind goes to bring you that which you truly desire.

Now you're on the right train.

[IF I ONLY KNEW THEN WHAT I KNOW NOW™]

LESSON 57

IS YOUR LIFE ANOTHER DREAM THAT ENDED WAY TOO SOON?

Most people go to their graves with their music still in them.
—Oliver Wendell Holmes

History is filled with people who have died way too soon and went to their graves with their music still in them.

Talented people, gifted people, special people, just like you, who always believed that one day they would finally use their incredibly special gifts and talents to help others and give them the kind of life they truly wanted, but they never did.

It was too late.

Time ran out, and their lives passed them by.

Will you be one of them?

THE LESSON TO BE LEARNED IS…

One of the big traps you can fall into is thinking that you will always have time to do what you truly want.

The truth is, all you have is today—right now. You don't have any guarantee that you will be here tomorrow, much less 10, 20, 30, 40 or more years from now.

Your life is much more than a dream that ended way too soon.

For no one at any time, anywhere, can steal your dreams or take them from you. As long as you're breathing, *now* is always the best time for you to live your dreams and have the life you truly want—regardless of your age.

And you don't need permission from anyone to do it.

Living the life you truly want is the gift you give to yourself and others. Live the life the way you want and you can rest assured, your dream will never end too soon.

[IF I ONLY KNEW THEN WHAT I KNOW NOW™]

LESSON 58

LISTEN TO WHAT THEY SAY THEY'RE NOT, BECAUSE THAT'S USUALLY WHAT THEY ARE

What a man does, tells us what he is.
—F. D. Huntington

Ever really to listen to people talk about themselves?

They give away the farm about themselves by revealing what they really are by emphatically stating what they're not.

Let me give you an example.

Someone may say, "I don't know why so many people I know think I'm materialistic." Yet, when you look at them, you see they are covered with jewelry, wear fancy clothes and shoes, drive luxury cars, live in expensive houses and just happen to slip into their conversations the vacation hot spot they just got back from and who they know, and the list goes on.

THE LESSON TO BE LEARNED IS…

Having nice things, living in a great home or traveling to exotic spots is perfectly wonderful. All those things are waiting for each of us to experience and have. However, many times when someone has to make a case for what they're not, that's usually a good indicator of what they really may be, so pay careful attention.

:: The Lessons of Life and What They're Trying to Teach You ::

The truth is, it's just natural for us to want to believe others when they tell us something. After all, we like giving others the benefit of the doubt. Yet, if you'll listen and watch them closely, they end up not hiding things very well. Their true colors come out.

And all you have to do is just sit back, listen and watch.

| LIFE'S WORDS OF WISDOM |

If you wish to be agreeable to society, you must agree to be taught many things which you know already.

—Johann Kaspar Lavater

[IF I ONLY KNEW THEN WHAT I KNOW NOW™]

LESSON 59

IT'S ALWAYS A GOOD TIME TO GET BACK TO BASICS

The more things change, the more they remain the same.
—French proverb

Seems that every day someone is inventing something to make our lives easier, better and more enjoyable.

As technology constantly changes, almost daily, computers, electronics and many other products are getting faster, doing more and costing less.

Then there are things we supposedly need.

Tune on the talk shows, read the paper, magazines or Internet and watch the latest infomercials and hear some expert or guru telling you that you need their system or program for the real success you've been missing in your life. And for just three easy payments you can change your life today.

THE LESSON TO BE LEARNED IS…

It's been said that the more things change, the more they remain the same.

That statement has never been more true than it is today.

Think about it.

Fashion and music that were hot 40 years ago are hot again today.

But in the endless sea of change, we have a deep desire to get back to basics. There's something good about getting back to the tried-and-true that has always worked for us.

Sure, it's great to try new things and keep those things you like and discard the rest; yet there's always something inside each of us that yearns to pull us back to the basics in every area of our life.

There's nothing fancy about the basics, and that's one of the reasons we like it so much.

And when it comes to changing anything in your life for the better, deep down you know that the basics are the time-tested, proven simplest way to do it.

Stay simple and stay with the basics, and they can help make you great.

| LIFE'S WORDS OF WISDOM |

If people only knew how hard I worked to gain mastery, it wouldn't seem so wonderful at all.

—Michelangelo

[IF I ONLY KNEW THEN WHAT I KNOW NOW™]

LESSON 60

WHATEVER HAPPENED TO THE MASTERS AND THE MASTERPIECES?

I offended God and mankind because my work didn't reach the quality it should have.
—Leonardo da Vinci

It's been said that during the past 50 years, more discoveries and information have been available to people than at any other time in history.

My question is, if that's true, then why haven't there been more masters and masterpieces?

The works of Shakespeare, Plato, Aristotle, Socrates, Leonardo da Vinci, Ralph Waldo Emerson, Beethoven, Vivaldi, Monet, Rembrandt and others are more valuable today than at any other time.

Works of the masters always are.

So with the incredible information superhighway of the Internet, lightning-fast computers, fuzzy-logic technology, artificial intelligence and everything else we have available at our fingertips today, why is it that so many people desire simply to be entertained and have little or no desire to create works and a life that will outlive them?

THE LESSON TO BE LEARNED IS...

In the long-ago ages of the masters and the masterpieces, all they had were simple colors (three to be exact), seven musical notes (same as today) and pen and paper.

:: The Lessons of Life and What They're Trying to Teach You ::

But look what they were able to create!

Yet inside you right now is the ability to be a master and create masterpieces.

Sure, you may not be a painter, poet, writer or musician, but the world doesn't judge greatness by simply being those.

It is how you use your incredible gifts and talents to affect those around you that makes your world, right now and the future, a better place because of your having passed this way.

Your mind is the same mind—in biological structure—as that of each master who created those masterpieces.

The big difference between you and them is how you have chosen to develop and use that great mind of yours.

Playing mind-numbing and growth-stunting activities like video games, watching endless hours of television or being entertained by surfing the Internet (unless of course you're gaining knowledge) doesn't help you tap into the deep reservoir of power that lies waiting for you within your mind.

Your mind is just like your muscles: If you don't use it and push it beyond what it's used to, it will not grow. Your mind grows and gets smarter and wiser only when you make it think.

As Benjamin Franklin so eloquently put it, "If everyone is thinking alike, then no one is thinking."

It's time to get back to those three colors and those seven notes and that pen and paper.

It's time to start creating your own masterpieces.

LESSON 61

IF IT ISN'T ONE THING, IT'S ANOTHER

Doubt whom you will, but never yourself.
—Christian Nestell Bovee

If you are looking for a quick way to stop enjoying the good things in your life, start believing that your life can't stay like this forever.

That's right.

Start looking around at the plight and frustration of so many others and start comparing your life to theirs. After all, you've worked so hard to get your life to go smoothly, yet others' lives are not; so of course something must be wrong with yours, right?

THE LESSON TO BE LEARNED IS…

The logic of what you just read sure sounds crazy, doesn't it?

But look at how many people follow it.

They allow doubt to creep into their mind, which is soon followed by the belief that such a wonderful life as theirs couldn't possibly last forever. Soon, new roots take hold and, without fail, their mind begins proving to them that they are right.

And it's even funny along the way.

That "knock on wood" thing people do, you know, when things are going good, is a sure tip-off that they're already living their lives on the edge of doubt and fear.

:: The Lessons of Life and What They're Trying to Teach You ::

I always wondered what in the world does wood or anything you knock on have to do with the thoughts you think, the actions you take and the success you achieve?

And then I found the answer: absolutely nothing, that's what!

Know the truth and the truth shall set you free; and that truth is, when it comes to having the life you want, you can have it and you can always have it if you desire and believe you can have it.

[IF I ONLY KNEW THEN WHAT I KNOW NOW™]

LESSON 62

OH, THOSE QUESTIONS

*You can make more friends in two months
by becoming more interested in other people,
than you can in two years
trying to get people interested in you.*

—Dale Carnegie

It's been said that the only true measure of a person's belief is their actions. Forget the words; actions are all that count.

And if you want to know if someone is truly interested and cares about you, all you have to do is listen.

Listen that is, to the questions they ask you.

For it is when someone truly cares about you, they'll ask you lots of questions about you and your life, dreams, goals, and so on.

The world is filled with people who love to have you ask them all kinds of questions about themselves. Yet, it's these same people who, after having talked about themselves for 98% of the time, may ask one or two passing questions about you—sort of obligatory, if you catch my drift.

These talkers—I believe folks used to called them yappers—are the unsure, insecure, self-centered, lack-of-direction, lack-of-purpose, poor-self-image, lack-of-goals type of people.

They will be your friend and even best buddy as long as you pump them up, pay attention to them and, by all means, ask them questions.

But stop asking them questions and see how much you both now have in common and how quickly the conversation dies out.

THE LESSON TO BE LEARNED IS…

Deeply personal and caring questions are so rarely asked anymore, and what a shame that is. For even more so today, people are begging inside that someone will take the time to talk with them in more than a superficial way.

Many people are so caught up into themselves that they feel their lives are the most important and that, quite naturally, other people *should* want to know about *them*.

But, ask a new friend or even older one, in-depth questions about themselves, their lives, careers, hopes, dreams, fears, joys, weaknesses, strengths or goals, and watch what happens.

You will be their hero and true friend and that rare someone who cares, unlike all the rest.

Sure, some people will be shocked when you do this; they may even express a little discomfort, but it won't last long.

One of the greatest things you can do is adopt the attitude that you're going to ask anyone the questions you want to ask them.

For your paths may never cross again. And by asking the questions that show you care, your life will be enriched from the knowledge gained, and their life will enriched from the caring you showed by making them feel important, even if only for a brief moment.

| LIFE'S WORDS OF WISDOM |

*If people were meant to be sheep,
they'd have four legs.*

[IF I ONLY KNEW THEN WHAT I KNOW NOW™]

LESSON 63

WATCH OUT FOR THE SHEEP

And be not conformed to this world: but be ye transformed by the renewing of your mind.
—Romans 12:2

Ever see a two-legged sheep?

Try picturing that in your mind.

What a funny sight.

Now, picture in your mind the sight of millions of people conforming to what family, friends and society think they should do, who they should be and how they should act.

Now you have a good idea of what a two-legged sheep looks and acts like.

THE LESSON TO BE LEARNED IS…

Never sell out, to anyone or anything, yourself or your dreams, goals and ambitions. And never, ever compromise your values, virtues, morals, beliefs, honor, word and your philosophy.

They're all you have.

So many people live in a "conform to perform" mode. It's the fear of what others may think about them that molds their behavior, beliefs and actions so they fit in, as uncomfortable and empty as that "fitting in" may be.

It's easy for you to do the same, but *don't you dare do it*.

Down the road, you will kick yourself over and over for becoming "one of them."

Don't join an "easy" crowd.

The great rewards in life go to those who are different, those who are daring and those who are bold.

Never set your goals too low, for it is the two-legged sheep that sets its goals too low and then underachieves.

Go where the demands are high and the expectations are strong.

Remember: If you don't need much, then you won't become much.

After all, the only things sheep need are food and water.

LESSON 64

THE EXCUSES FOR NOT BEING, NOT DOING AND NOT HAVING

We have forty million reasons for failure but not a single excuse.

—Rudyard Kipling

Excuses are like opinions; seems everybody else has one when it comes to not doing, becoming or having that which they want.

And be on the lookout.

Nowadays, wherever you go, there's an epidemic plaguing the world. It's called *excusitis,* and it's a condition brought on by inflammation of the "I can't" gland.

THE LESSON TO BE LEARNED IS...

Failure always needs an alibi, and success never needs an excuse.

Every time you tell yourself you're going to do something and you don't do it, you lose power. Your subconscious mind listens to everything you tell it, so when you don't follow through on that which you say you will, you send a powerful message to your mind that it's okay to not do and achieve that which you say you will. Each time you do that, it becomes easier and easier to do it the next time and the next time.

Some of the excuses people use to describe the cause of their misery, lack of success, unwise choices and inaction are:

"My real love is this, but I should do this."

"We'll, I'll just have to wait and see what happens."

"I don't want to get too excited before it happens, because I don't want to be disappointed if it doesn't."

"I couldn't care less about the money."

"If I had the money, there's nothing more I'd like to do than help people out."

"I've been so busy that I haven't had enough time to call or email."

"I'd really like to start my own business, but I don't have the money, education, connections, experience, ..."

"I'm just waiting for God's will, and if He wants it to happen, it will happen."

Let me make an observation on that last statement for a moment.

Many well-intentioned people make that statement and really believe it; they're so busy waiting for God, they don't take action.

It's a bit like the story of the man who was broke and asked God to help him win the lottery. After weeks of waiting, the man was frustrated and finally called to God, "Dear God, I thought you would help me!" God replied, "Hey, the least you could do is buy a ticket."

Studying the lives of successful people can reveal many things.

Among them, they believed God helps those who help themselves.

If the desire is placed in your heart, then that's a strong indicator of the next thing you need to do.

And remember, you must first take action to make whatever you want happen. Whatever you do, give it all your best; then give it to God and let Him do the rest.

Throw away the excuses.

It's time to take responsibility for everything that has happened to you—past, present and future.

As William Ernest Henley once penned, "You are the master of your fate, the captain of your soul."

Live by the attitude that "If I don't start, it's absolutely certain I won't arrive."

LESSON 65

THE POWER AND EMOTION OF A HANDWRITTEN LETTER

The word that is heard perishes, but the letter that is written remains.

—Proverb

The handwritten letter. Countless lives have been changed because of them.

Throughout history, people have loved to receive them. There's something special about a handwritten letter that can't be duplicated by anything else. Email and texting don't even come close.

Handwritten letters help crystallize thought and allow you to share your thoughts and ideas better than spoken words. A letter from you allows the reader to focus specifically on what you're saying. They can read and re-read your letter many times and pick up words, phrases and meanings they may have overlooked the first time.

A handwritten letter speaks volumes that you care enough to take time out and express your thoughts, in a rare way that few others do today.

THE LESSON TO BE LEARNED IS...

Go the opposite direction of what most people do and write a handwritten response. The excitement of sending a letter and having someone receive it and read it, plus the anticipation and surprise of their receiving a letter from you, are among life's most simple joys.

Think of it.

Which would touch you more: a typed form letter, email or text, or a completely personalized handwritten letter created just for you?

LESSON 66

TELL ME ABOUT YOUR PERFECT DAY

If you can't describe it, then how will you ever live it?

That's an awakening thought.

After all, who has time to think about a perfect day when so much of a person's life is spent just getting through this one with minimal frustration and as few problems as possible?

The harsh reality is that people who think like that are bound, for the rest of their lives, to keep going through the same old same old and getting the same old same old. If you've been one of them, I ask you: Is that good news?

THE LESSON TO BE LEARNED IS...

Can you tell me about your perfect day?

Where would you live?

What kind of relationship would you have?

What kind of career would you have?

What time would you get up?

What would you do and whom would you meet with during the day?

What kinds of activities would you be involved in?

If you can't answer these questions and many others about your perfect day, how on earth will you ever live it and enjoy it?

The truth is, you can't and you won't, unless you decide that you can have whatever kind of day you want and you will not accept anything less. Period.

So many people can't answer those questions because *they're too busy trying to make a living to make a life.*

For it is a fact that *if you don't start believing in, and living, the life you want to live, you will continue to believe the life you are now living.*

Only you can live your perfect day. Only you can give yourself that wonderful gift. Only you know what that perfect day is for you.

The best way to have the future you want is to create it.

LESSON 67

YOU ARE MOVING IN THE DIRECTION OF YOUR PICTURES

Our brain and nervous system cannot tell the difference between a real experience or one which is vividly imagined.
—Dr. Maxwell Maltz

The mind doesn't know the difference between a real or an imagined event.

The late Dr. Maxwell Maltz made that observation in his inspiring classic book, *Psycho-Cybernetics*. And to this day, that statement rings loud and true.

You see, you, I and every other human being thinks in words and pictures. Yet, it's when the mental picture of something or someone is placed with words that we're caused to feel the emotions we do.

That's good news.

THE LESSON TO BE LEARNED IS...

It's good news because if you can change your mental pictures, you can change the emotion you feel with it and the result you will get.

The key is to create new pictures of how you want to be.

See yourself as more confident, more successful, outgoing, able to get along with anyone and everyone and being really happy and fulfilled.

Now, do that for every other area in your life, be it relationships, career, sports, hobbies or anything else. By

:: The Lessons of Life and What They're Trying to Teach You ::

giving your brain new pictures to look at, you're also able to paste on to those pictures any emotion you want to feel.

That is tremendously empowering for you, because now, with the new picture and positive and powerful emotions that only support you in your goals and dreams, you'll be able to have the kind of life you truly want to have and do it much faster than you may have imagined possible.

LESSON 68

THE BODY YOU HAVE IS THE BODY YOU WANT

Where the mind goes, the body follows.

Take a good look at your body.

What you see in the mirror is exactly the kind of body you believe you should have. After all, it fits perfectly with your mental picture of the body you think you should have.

That can be a rude awakening for people.

After all, how can they be so dissatisfied with their bodies if, all along, that is the body they will always go back to after the diet program fails and the exercise program gets too boring?

THE LESSON TO BE LEARNED IS…

It all goes back to those mental pictures you've been giving yourself.

You see, your subconscious mind is like a faithful servant that never questions the commands or the mental pictures you give it. Its only job is to make the words you tell yourself and the mental pictures you give it come true, day in, day out, 365 days a year and for the rest of your life.

If you want to look and feel different, you must first change the mental picture of how you look now to how you want to look before you rush out to buy the latest diet book, get a personal trainer, take the hottest new exercise

:: The Lessons of Life and What They're Trying to Teach You ::

class and start throwing out all those "unhealthy" foods in your pantry for "health" foods.

When you first begin changing those mental pictures of you, your mind will keep asking you and raising doubts if those new pictures are really something you honestly think you can achieve.

That's perfectly normal, for the job of the subconscious has always been to bring you that which is in perfect harmony with what you've always pictured and told yourself. When some new picture or new commands and emotions are given to it, it first wants to reject them because they are different from what it's been used to.

The key is to keep feeding your mind those new mental pictures of you *already* having the body you want.

That's right.

Act as if you already have it.

For *the more you act is if, the quicker you will soon become.*

Feel the emotions that go along with that new body and the confidence, energy, and great feelings.

It won't be long before your subconscious mind will reject the old image of you and lock on to the new image all the behaviors and results that match it.

LESSON 69

IS YOUR LIFE AN "I CAN'T WAIT TO GET OVER THIS" EVENT?

Life is to be enjoyed, not endured.

Seems everywhere you turn so many people are unhappy and frustrated.

It's as if this thing they were given called "their life" is looked at as a prison sentence with the majority of their lives' being spent trying to get out of the unhappiness that they've created by their own thinking.

Why does life have to be perceived as so hard when in essence it can be so easy, so fulfilling and so much fun?

THE LESSON TO BE LEARNED IS…

If your life is an "I can't wait to get over this" event, then it's time you woke up to the truth.

Chances are, you are a responder and are affected by your environment instead of being an activator and taking charge and affecting your environment. For the more control you have over your life, the more secure and happy you feel.

That control begins with your decision to know exactly what you want for your life and taking focused action until you achieve it.

Unless you do so, you're bound to go through life merely trying to dodge the obstacles and jump over the hurdles that the circumstances of life throw your way.

:: The Lessons of Life and What They're Trying to Teach You ::

You've got but one life to live, and it is right now.

Think back to how much precious time you've wasted and experiences you've allowed yourself to miss, just because your mind was focused on getting over a particular event so you could feel better about your future.

It's time to make your life an "I can't wait to experience it!" event.

| LIFE'S WORDS OF WISDOM |

Make conditions serve you.
Think strongly.
Attempt fearlessly.
Accomplish masterfully.

—Anonymous

[IF I ONLY KNEW THEN WHAT I KNOW NOW™]

LESSON 70

CIRCUMSTANCES? I MAKE MY OWN!

People are always blaming their circumstances for what they are. I don't believe in circumstances. The people who get on in this world are the people who get up and look for the circumstances they want, and, if they can't find them, make them.
—George Bernard Shaw

Make your own circumstances.

That sounds too easy. It can't possibly be true.

Can it?

A lot of people think it can't be true, so they don't even try. To them, life should be difficult, because if something in life is easy, well then, someone else would already be doing it.

Yet look at the lives of those who made this country great, did great things, inspired others and made a mark in this world, and you will see, without fail, that each of these people were trailblazers, pioneers and visionaries.

They were people, just like you, who wouldn't accept a life of mediocrity and of just getting by constantly going through the motions and the endless going-through-the-going-through stage.

THE LESSON TO BE LEARNED IS...

Take a good look at your life right now.

Look at the problems you have today.

Are they the very same problems you had 1, 2 or even 3 years ago?

If they are, it could be you haven't grasped the age-old truth, *if you keep doing what you're doing, you're bound to keep getting the same things you've been getting.*

Look at why you haven't made the changes you must make to rid your life of those problems. Once and for all, give up the fairytale that someday soon, someone is going to knock on your door and make your life all better.

You are the only one who has the power to choose what's best for you.

Choose to not take any new action or learn from past experiences, and your life will continue to give you what you've been getting.

But choose wisely, and you will be rewarded.

LESSON 71

BALANCING THE TRIANGLE

Simplicity is an exact medium between too little and too much.

—Sir Joshua Reynolds

Life is much like a triangle.

In order to feel a good sense of balance, you need to have equal development of the spiritual, emotional and physical parts of your life.

Yet many people do not, and as a result their pyramid of balance and happiness in their lives topples over because too much attention and focus is placed on one side to the exclusion of the others. Unbalanced life = unbalanced pyramid = unhappy and unfulfilled life.

THE LESSON TO BE LEARNED IS…

It takes many things to make up who you are. You have lots of interests, hobbies and desires. Just as importantly, you have incredible gifts, talents and abilities that are only yours to use to bless and help the lives of others.

Yet unless you spend equal time developing your spiritual, emotional and physical sides, you will always be unbalanced and searching outside yourself for the answer to your uneasiness.

But other people can't give it to you.

Material things can never give it you.

And a change in jobs or where you live can't give you the total balance you crave.

Seems that your soul has a mind of its own, and it knows how to lead you to that which you need for the balance you seek.

Listen to your inner guidance and follow its message. It will lead you to what you need to create the triangle of balance in all parts of your life.

LESSON 72

THE POWER OF FORGIVENESS—IT'S TIME TO SET YOURSELF FREE

"I can forgive, but I cannot forget" is only another way of saying "I will not forgive."

—Anonymous

It's a strange quirk about human nature to hold a grudge against someone and not let it go.

Our perception that someone has done something wrong to us, makes us feel in control and in power over that person.

So we hold the anger inside, just waiting for that other person to somehow magically realize what they did to hurt us and come begging us for forgiveness.

Yet rarely does that happen.

In fact, many times the other person has no idea how the words they said, or how the actions they did or did not do, hurt us and caused us all that anger in the first place.

So here we are, walking around for much too long with bitterness, resentment and hurt, and all it has done is cause us discomfort, a body that is continually flooded with chemicals from all the stress, and eventually a host of other physical, mental and spiritual maladies that do nothing but squeeze the very life from us.

It's time to set yourself free.

THE LESSON TO BE LEARNED IS…

Forgiveness is always in your power and is a completely selfish act that you do for yourself and others. When you forgive, you set yourself free from all the emotions and negativity that have caused you so much unhappiness for so long.

People have found all kinds of ways to forgive others.

Spiritually minded folks pray that the person who hurt them be blessed. That's a powerful way to neutralize and eliminate any anger.

Then, there's a great idea simply called the letter.

There are two ways you can use this.

First, on a piece of paper write down everything that the other person said or did to hurt you in any way. At the end of the letter, tell them that you unconditionally and freely forgive them.

Then either send the letter off to them or, if it's a relationship you want to end but want closure and peace, write the letter, forgive them and then tear up or burn the letter.

You won't believe how great you'll feel by doing this.

My friend, many people have said on their deathbeds that life is too short not to forgive anyone for anything.

As one grows older in years and wisdom, this truth becomes more and more clear.

I'm saying forgive everyone today. Anger and hurt are a high price to pay for stealing your happiness, peace of mind and quality and length of your life.

:: The Lessons of Life and What They're Trying to Teach You ::

LESSON 73

BREAK FREE FROM THE SHACKLES OF THE PAST

Successful people talk about the future; mediocre people talk about the present and losers talk about the past. I focus on the future because that's where I expect to spend the rest of my life.

—Anonymous

Pick someone you know or may not know and listen to what they talk about.

Do they talk about the past, present or future? You can tell a lot about that person—what they believe, the kind of life they expect to have—simply by listening to the time-frame and subject of their conversation.

The world is filled with people who live in the past.

The old saying that if you don't learn from the past, you're bound to repeat it, is so true. Those who reminisce about the past will talk about the good ol' days and perhaps all the things that are wrong with people and society today. For these folks, the future and present are all filtered through the filter called the past, and their decisions to act and experience new things or the same old things are based on their past reference system.

Then there are those who speak in the present and about today. Yet many of these people neither believe in nor have set any goals for their lives. They merely react to whatever it is that life happens to throw their way today.

It's time to stop letting your past be your future.

THE LESSON TO BE LEARNED IS…

The future always has always belonged and always will belong to the visionaries.

The visionaries are the dreamers and doers. They make what they dream, picture and envision become realities because of theire unshakable belief in creating a future they want.

Where there is no vision, the people do perish. And where there is only a vision of the past and present, the people waste their lives and this precious and priceless thing called time.

Remember, if you are not thinking about your future today, you're no closer to having the kind of life you haven't dreamed for yourself tomorrow.

For today truly is yesterday's tomorrow.

The people who do great things have learned from the past but live in the present while making every action they take today count for something for achieving their vision of the future they want tomorrow.

Be one of them.

| LIFE'S WORDS OF WISDOM |

What the mind of man can conceive and believe, it can achieve.

—Napoleon Hill

LESSON 74

IN YOUR MIND, THERE'S NO SPACE AND TIME

The greatest discovery of my generation is that a human being can alter his life by altering his attitudes of mind.
—William James

Sounds a little heady to me. Perhaps an explanation is in order.

What many people don't realize is that the mind doesn't know time limitations or whether some event has happened, is happening or will happen. To the mind, it is all happening right now in the present.

I want you to think of a negative experience that happened some time ago in your past. Doesn't it seem like it just happened yesterday? Yet, this event may have happened 10, 20, 30 or more years ago.

Now, try thinking of a past positive event. You'll probably find that it's much harder for the mind to do, because of how our minds have been conditioned toward negativity by friends, family and society.

It's much the same way when we try to see the future the way we want it. It's like our minds are stuck in quicksand and want to stay focused on the past or present situations and problems. But it doesn't have to be that way.

THE LESSON TO BE LEARNED IS...

The key to getting your mind focused on positive things is using its ability to view things in the present and giving it new pictures, words and emotions as if those things are happening right now for you—even if they aren't right now.

You might ask, wouldn't that be telling yourself a lie?

As Zig Ziglar likes to say, "All you're doing is simply telling the truth in advance."

And it's true.

You must give your mind the mental picture of your having already achieved that goal or dream that you want, so it can make the necessary changes in your life for you to actually do it.

Of course, you do recall by now that your mind can't tell the difference between a real or imagined experience. So keeping your mind focused on only that which you want and off of the things you don't want, is one sure way to make whatever you want to happen, happen.

LESSON 75

YOUR PARENTS DID THE BEST THEY KNEW

For some people, it takes fifty years to get over their first five.
—Anonymous

This phrase "dysfunctional family" has really become the buzzword as of late.

Seems that most everyone's troubles and lack of drive and success in life can be traced directly back to their parents for not giving them the tools they needed to become self-actualized, fully functioning adults.

Time for a wake-up call.

Name me one person, that's right, just one person, who came from a perfect family.

Having a bit of trouble, are we?

Don't worry; I can't think of one either.

In this world of blaming our woeful inadequacies on good old Mom and Dad, I'm reminded of a quote about parenting that says, "Parenting is simply the passing down of insanity from one generation to the next."

What do you think?

THE LESSON TO BE LEARNED IS…

You, I and everyone else got their first lessons about relationships from our parents or some other authority figure, if Mom and Dad weren't around. What you take into your adult relationships is in large part based on the examples you saw when you were growing up.

:: The Lessons of Life and What They're Trying to Teach You ::

Now, you have a choice.

In fact, for many people, from the age of 18 on, the life you have is the life you've made, and no one else is to blame. Of course, your childhood experiences can stay with you for a lifetime, if that is what you've decided to keep and use as your reference system for evaluating, judging and acting upon the choices you are presented with each day.

Or, you can choose to let go of the things from your past that aren't working or are causing you pain and choose to replace those things with beliefs, attitudes and actions that do work better for you.

Leave Mom and Dad out of it.

How they raised you was the best they could with what they knew how.

They weren't given all the best tools and examples to learn from when they were growing up, so how in the world did you expect them to pull the rabbit out of the hat when it came to raising you?

Sure it might have been better if they had done this or they hadn't done that, but whose life wouldn't have been?

But they weren't perfect. They simply did what they thought they could. Understand them, forgive them if you hold any grudges and learn from their example.

LESSON 76

YOU LEARN BY WATCHING

Instead of saying that man is the creature of circumstances, say that man is the architect of circumstances.

—Thomas Carlyle

Humans are amazing creatures.

Of all the things that were given life, it's been said that only humans have complete control over their thoughts and possess the power to choose and not be driven by instinct like animals.

Yet, like animals, people learn many of their behaviors from watching. That is, watching their parents, siblings, friends and others.

In essence, people are masters at something called mirroring; watching someone or something and duplicating that behavior or action, many times without even a thought as to why.

The problem with this is that many of the behaviors, beliefs and actions learned while growing up can actually hold people back later on life.

So what do many people do when that happens? Blame their spouses, boyfriends, girlfriends, friends, parents and anyone else but themselves.

:: The Lessons of Life and What They're Trying to Teach You ::

THE LESSON TO BE LEARNED IS…

The behaviors you have are the behaviors you've chosen to keep, whether they are wise or unwise, good or bad, happy or sad.

When you were growing up, you may have had pressure to conform to the expectations of those who were the keepers of the house, but as an adult, it's an entirely different story.

How many times have you heard someone say, "She's just like her mom" or "He's just like his dad"?

Why are they that way?

Is it a genetic thing that can't be changed?

Chances are it's because they've chosen to hold on to those limiting beliefs, fears, doubts, worries and negativity that they saw in their parents that their parents probably never fully realized they had.

The great news is that you don't have to be like anyone except yourself.

Being anything or anyone else is just a lie.

If you enjoy mirroring others so much, allow yourself to mirror those of the truly great and rare people who are filled with love and command respect and honor wherever they go and from whomever they meet.

See yourself as truly great, and very soon the world will too.

[IF I ONLY KNEW THEN WHAT I KNOW NOW™]

LESSON 77

WHEN IT COMES TO PEOPLE, I'M POSITIVE THAT MOST ARE NEGATIVE

Nothing is easier than fault-finding; no talent, no self-denial, no brains, no character are required to set up in the grumbling business.
—Robert West

I'm absolutely amazed at how many people are negative.

These are the gloom-and-doomers who can more quickly remind you of the things that didn't work, than the things that did.

The same people who always have a gripe, an ache or a pain, who are constantly struggling financially and who look for the things that could wrong instead of go right.

When you get down to it, people can really be divided into two groups: the malevolents and the benevolents.

The malevolents are those who are angry at life and think life is basically a struggle and unfair.

The benevolents see life as basically good and fair, provided you do the things and take the action necessary to have the things you want and do the things you want to do.

THE LESSON TO BE LEARNED IS...

Life is like a magnet.

:: The Lessons of Life and What They're Trying to Teach You ::

Positive people think positive thoughts and tend to attract the people and circumstances in their lives that are positive, fulfilling, happy and successful.

Like attracts like.

The most important power you have is the power to choose.

That's right. No one can influence or make you choose something unless you give them that power.

You can choose to be negative and live a life that attracts problems and heartache and repels the good from you, or you can choose to be positive.

Once you know the difference, I'm positive you won't choose to be negative.

LESSON 78

JEALOUSY AND GOSSIP, THE WORLD'S FAVORITE SPORTS

There is a sure way to avoid criticism: be nothing and do nothing.

—Anonymous

Wherever you go, whatever country you visit, you'll find that people love to talk about other people. It's as if gossip has become a worldwide pastime. Yet good-natured harmless gossip is one thing. Gossip motivated by jealousy is quite another.

Even in the sweetest of people, jealousy can be a green-eyed monster that consumes many of their thoughts and motivates many of their actions.

They feel threatened by the perceived threat from a co-worker, business partner or friend who they believe is out to get them or their job or position for whatever imaginary reason they've allowed themselves to believe. The joking and the kidding begin as just good-natured gossip on the surface, but deep down it quickly turns into something more negative.

Life is filled with dramas of people being let go from a job, causing relationships to be changed and ruined and preventing or aborting their potential as an employee—all because someone in management became jealous of that person's drive, ambition, great attitude, ability to get along with others and ability to do a great job.

Countless dollars and potential have been wasted, all because of the fragile egos of the Mr. or Ms. Eggshells.

Seems that companies, the very ones whose management complain about worker morale, productivity and profits, are the same ones that keep these human-potential destroyers in power and turn a deaf ear and a blind eye when one of the loyal, committed and caring employees comes to them with legitimate concerns about their future, their co-workers and that of the company management professes to love.

THE LESSON TO BE LEARNED IS...

The one thing you can't control is what other people say or think about you.

If you're looking for acceptance, understand that few people will give it to you unconditionally.

And that's okay.

One of the greatest stories I ever heard was that of an older man who was being introduced to someone for the first time. The person introducing him said, "I've known this man for over 50 years, and not once during that time have I, nor anyone I know who knows him, heard him say anything negative about anyone." My, oh my. How easy it sounds, yet how hard it is.

Many times in your life, you may be faced with situations and have to adapt yourself to conditions that may at first seem unfavorable to you, all because of someone else's jealousy and gossip.

This is human nature.

Stay strong and simply stay the course, no matter how tough it is, for whatever you're faced with will soon pass and the hardship will be over.

Yet, after the smoke clears and things have settled down for you, what will remain are the side-effects that the person who wronged you must face from the words they said and the actions they took.

Some call it karma.

Others know it to be one of the unchangeable laws of life, that life is like a boomerang; what you throw out comes back to you.

Though the results of someone's actions may not come back right way, be assured that those results will be returned to them on a much greater scale than what was originally given out.

Reason enough for anyone to stop the gossip and end the jealousy.

LESSON 79

YOU CAN BECOME AN EXPERT

Nature arms each man with some faculty which enables him to do easily some feat impossible to any other, and thus makes him necessary to society.
—Ralph Waldo Emerson

If you want to be a success, becoming an expert can be your surest and quickest route.

In this fast-paced, information-overloaded world, those who will write their own tickets for success are those who are specialists. The jack-of-all-trades-and-master-of-none is great for around the house, but this person won't cut it in the business world.

People demand specialists.

You probably do too.

The best doctors, mechanics, electricians, plumbers, engineers and so many others are always in top demand and get the best jobs and top dollar for what they do.

They should.

After all, they did what the majority of others chose not to do and did whatever it took to be the best in their fields.

The good news is—and this may surprise you—becoming a specialist is much easier than you think.

THE LESSON TO BE LEARNED IS…

I'm going to tell you about something called the 15-Minute Solution, and it has the power to change your life forever.

So many people complain that they have no time to do the things they say they want to do, like take an extra class or get more education to become a specialist. Yet, upon closer look, these people are time wasters and don't understand the 15-Minute Solution.

Think about it: Fifteen minutes sure doesn't sound like much time now, does it? Yet, if you will get up 15 minutes earlier every morning or go to bed 15 minutes later every night, those 15 minutes can change your life.

So what, you may ask, will you do with those extra 15 minutes?

You will pick one subject you really love. One for which you may have always dreamed what it would be like if you could really do that in life and get paid great money for it.

Each day you will study about that subject.

You will read, listen to and watch whatever you can that has to do with that subject. You will uncover things about that subject that you never knew, and soon you will uncover things that others never knew.

In a very short time, you will become an expert on that subject, a real authority others will seek.

You will have transformed yourself from someone who does the same thing, day after day, to one who loves what they do, knows more about the subject than anybody else and has become a specialist in high demand who can command top dollar and working conditions.

Yes, 15 minutes doesn't sound like much time, but think about it. If you study the subject you love for just 15 minutes a day, in 30 days you will have studied 7.5 hours.

That may not sound like much, but in six months you will have studied the subject you love for 45 hours; that's 45 hours of concentrated study on one subject, and it's the subject you love.

In just one year, you will have filled your mind with a whopping 91 hours of specific, tightly focused study on your favorite subject—far more than any college course.

And this is only with an extra 15 minutes each day.

Study for 20 or 30 minutes or more a day and watch how fast you become the specialist you always dreamed of.

LESSON 80

THE GIVE AND TAKE OF LOVE

Our success and happiness in life is dependent on two things: how much we love and serve others.

Each of us has a communication problem.

The problem is knowing how we give and receive love and how we communicate that love and those needs to others and how well they communicate those same things to us.

THE LESSON TO BE LEARNED IS…

First of all, understand how you like to give and receive love.

You may be one who likes hearing the words of love and that may be how you let others know that you love them.

Then again, you may be one who expresses love in your actions, by doing things for others and having others do things for you.

Of course, words and actions can take many forms, and understanding which form you like best and like to receive best will go a long way in preventing misunderstandings and hurt and giving you the feedback you need to let you know that you're wanted, needed and appreciated.

Even if you don't know the other person well enough to know how they give and receive love, never, ever, refuse any help, gift, act of kindness or nice words spoken to you.

:: The Lessons of Life and What They're Trying to Teach You ::

Never block the channel of love the other person wants to express to you in whatever way they feel best. They're reaching out to you and this may be a hard thing for them to do.

Blocking someone else's desire to do nice things for you or minimizing what they say to you only takes away the other's sense of validation and feelings of honestly expressing themselves with the love they feel for you in their heart.

Accept what someone else says or does for you, just as you want them to accept unconditionally what you say and do for them.

It's the give and take of the magic of love.

LESSON 81

MONEY IS THE ROOT OF MUCH GOODNESS

*Money makes a good person better and
a bad person worse.*

—Anonymous

The phrase so often misquoted by people is that "money is the root of all evil."

For those biblically minded, they know it's far from the truth, for the biblical injunction they misquote actually states that the *love* of money is the root of evil.

I don't know about you, but evil is a pretty vague term that means a lot of different things to different people.

The point I believe these misquoting people make is that when money becomes your god, to the exclusion of forsaking relationships with family, friends and loved ones, then the pursuit of money can be a big problem.

You see, money is only a medium of exchange.

It's inert matter that cannot think or breathe.

Yet, it's the importance we assign to it that determines if it becomes our life or rather, gives us more life.

THE LESSON TO BE LEARNED IS…

More money will only make more of what you already are.

As one billionaire put it, "People who say that their life would be far easier if only they had money, obviously don't have money."

:: The Lessons of Life and What They're Trying to Teach You ::

The key to bringing more money into your life, after you've used your gifts, talents and abilities to help others by increasing the amount of service to them, is to be generous with your money.

One of the immediate ways you can see how this works is to become a great tipper.

The next time you get great service in a restaurant or someone does some work for you, give them a big tip and watch how they respond. You will have just made their day, and in doing so you will have ensured that the next time they see you they will treat you royally.

But the big benefit is what you don't see after you've finished or when you leave.

You just made sure that the next person the person you tipped encounters will get a big smile and great service. Just think what would happen if we all did that.

Once you get into the habit of being great tipper, you're not going to want to stop.

One great way to bring more wealth and happiness into your life is to go a little out of your way to do something for someone else who doesn't even expect it. It's that spirit of giving purely for the sake of giving, and expecting nothing in return.

The old adage that the more you give, the more you will receive is one of life's great truths and rewards.

| LIFE'S WORDS OF WISDOM |

To know the mighty works of God; to comprehend His wisdom and majesty and power; to appreciate, in degree, the wonderful working of His laws, surely all this must be a pleasing and acceptable mode of worship to the Most High, to whom ignorance can not be more grateful than knowledge.

—Copernicus

LESSON 82

GET PLUGGED BACK INTO YOUR POWER SOURCE

To believe in the things you can see and touch is no belief at all; but to believe in the unseen is a triumph and a blessing.

—Abraham Lincoln

It's been said that spiritual power is the great unseen. And it's for that reason that many people blow it off and neglect its importance.

We tend to be believers, that is, in whatever our five senses (taste, touch, smell, sight and hearing) signal back to us. After all, these are things we experience daily, so naturally they're going to be easiest to relate to and believe.

Yet the greatest of people through the ages have recognized that the unseen is the greatest of all powers.

THE LESSON TO BE LEARNED IS…

Think of yourself like an electrical appliance with a long power cord and a battery inside.

When you're plugged into a power source, you can run at maximum power and your battery is continually being recharged; so if, by chance, your power cord gets unplugged, your battery will allow you to continue to run, but only for a short time.

That's what happens to you when you get unplugged from your power source—your life force.

Despite all your beliefs that you can do it all without any help from a higher power, you become one who experiences a constant power drain—it could be slow or fast—because you're not being recharged from your power source.

In a short time, you become burned out, lazy, lethargic and uncaring, and you feel hopeless and discouraged.

That's why quiet time is so important.

It's only in those still quiet moments that you are able to hear that still small voice from within, giving you direction and wisdom about your life, its direction, answers to your problems and the opportunity to recharge your mental, physical and spiritual batteries.

Forget whatever name you call it.

Think of the miracle of your life, of animals and plants, of the great oceans and mountains, of the sun, moon and the stars and of all of nature. Realize that the same power source that created all those things also created you.

Get connected back into the source of all goodness, power, strength, wisdom, knowledge, love and direction for your life.

Your power source is waiting.

Waiting for you to get plugged in again.

LESSON 83

PAYING YOUR DO'S

When it comes to giving, look at how many people stop at nothing.

—Anonymous

Earlier we had talked about how people give and receive love.

Most people enjoy receiving things from others.

Some people really like kind words and compliments, the things they can replay over and over in their mind.

When I was growing up, our family had a big vegetable garden, and one of the things my mother and father loved to do was to give vegetables away to family, friends and even strangers.

They purposely planted more than they could ever use, just so they would have enough to give to others.

Everyone loved receiving their vegetables.

But no more than Mom and Dad loved giving them. That was a powerful lesson to me about the how giving impacts the lives of others.

THE LESSON TO BE LEARNED IS…

So what kinds of things do people like to receive?

Well, some of the all-time favorites are flowers, cards, thank-you notes and handwritten letters; telephone calls, compliments and words of encouragement regarding your belief in them; the asking of caring questions specifically about their life; the act of volunteering to help them, giving them the message that you'd like to do something to make their life easier and more meaningful; things you no longer need that they can use; small gifts and tokens of appreciation; and, of course, your taking the first step by reaching out to them and creating the friendship you both want.

LESSON 84

THE LOST ART OF LISTENING

You have two ears and one mouth, which is proof enough that you should listen twice as much as you talk.
—Anonymous

People love to talk.

It can it be said with reasonable certainty that some people live to talk, especially about the most important subject in the world—themselves.

Maybe we're all guilty when it comes to pretending to listen to what someone else says, when all the while we are merely hoping that they will hurry up and finish what they're saying so we can tell them what we're thinking.

Most of the time we are not really listening; we're just waiting for the other to finish talking so we can begin.

The late human relations teacher Dale Carnegie was a big believer in keeping your conversations focused on the other person's interests and, once you ask that person questions about those interests, keeping your mouth shut until they have finished talking.

And it works with uncanny accuracy and predictable results.

For it only takes a short while of the other person talking about themselves that they will immediately stop and make a statement like, "Geez, it seems I've been doing all the talking. Why don't you tell me about you?"

So glad you asked!

THE LESSON TO BE LEARNED IS…

People won't listen to you until they are ready to hear what you say.

The old saying, "People don't care how much you know until they know how much you care," is so very true.

The way to show them you care is to ask questions about them and then listen to their responses.

It can be frustrating to pour out your heart and soul to someone, only to see that they aren't listening or, if they are, that what you say really doesn't matter or impact them much. Sort of like they hear what you're saying, but they're not *listening*.

Many people practice selective deafness; they tune out what you say and the message you're trying to impart, because what you're saying is not what they want to hear at this particular time in their life. Yet tomorrow or next week it could be an entirely different story.

Listening is a lost art that, once mastered, will endear you to become a friend to all.

You'll be amazed at how people will tell you how much they enjoyed talking with you, even if all you did was listen.

After all, one of the greatest needs of anyone is the need to feel wanted, needed and appreciated. Giving your undivided attention to others by listening to them helps fill that void in their life. The age-old advice, "talking is sharing and listening is caring," is about as true as it gets.

| LIFE'S WORDS OF WISDOM |

If you have knowledge,
let others light their candles at it.

—Margaret Fuller

[IF I ONLY KNEW THEN WHAT I KNOW NOW™]

LESSON 85

MENTORS—YOUR GREATEST TEACHERS

If you are successful remember that somewhere, sometime, someone gave you a lift or an idea that started you in the right direction. Remember, also, that you are indebted to life until you help some less fortunate person, just as you were helped.

—Napoleon Hill

Many people grew up in less–than-ideal environments for success.

Maybe it was the poor conditions of their country, the hardships of having to support a family at an early age, living within a single-parent or no-parent family, the influence of drugs, gangs and the inner city or an environment that fostered helplessness, negativity and poverty.

So why is it that, despite the seemingly overwhelming odds stacked against them, many of these people become incredible successes?

Of course, they each must hold an undying belief that nothing can stop them from having the kind of life—a better life—that they truly desire.

Yet, even with that unshakable belief, people still need motivation, education and an understanding of the success tools that will enable anyone, anywhere, to achieve that which they so deeply desire.

So tell me: Besides college and books, where does one find such sources of inspiration?

:: The Lessons of Life and What They're Trying to Teach You ::

Mentors.

Mentors are those people who impact your life in a positive way.

They change your life by helping you see and pull out the greatness that lies within you.

They teach you the shortcuts and help you avoid the pitfalls on your road to success.

The great news is that there are mentors waiting for you right now.

THE LESSON TO BE LEARNED IS...

Pick any interest you have, and you can find a mentor who is doing it and can show you how you can do it too.

Doesn't matter what it is. For there is someone, somewhere, right now who is an expert on that subject and who would be happy to share their strategies for success with you.

You see, many successful people live by the attitude that they got where they are with a lot of belief and hard work, and with help from someone who believed enough in them to take a chance.

Now that they've achieved success, they want to return the favor to someone else.

That someone could be you.

Remember, 30 minutes of talk with a wise man or woman is worth more than a month's study of books.

And even though they may have great wealth and power, mentors understand where you are coming from, for they too came from humble beginnings.

You will find that the most successful people are also the easiest to approach and talk to.

They understand fear, doubt, worry and frustration; but they have mastered them, and by doing so they make life pay on their own terms.

Mentors can show you how to do the same.

Seek them.

Call them.

Write them.

Meet them.

Learn from them.

Your life and theirs will never be the same.

LESSON 86

A MODEL FOR SUCCESS

Talent learns from others,
a genius from himself.
—Arnold Schoenberg

Just as we talked about learning from mentors, the next step is to apply what you learn. For knowledge is only potential power until it is applied in specific ways for a specific result.

If you are inspired by a mentor and would like to attain a similar level of achievement, start practicing something called modeling.

Think of modeling like this: If someone has achieved certain talent or skill that you feel you could to, simply model that person's actions, beliefs and behavior and you can achieve it too.

THE LESSON TO BE LEARNED IS...

Of course, just watching a person do something can give you valuable lessons on how you can do the same thing.

But it needs to go beyond that.

You need to understand their thought process, beliefs and the words (the internal success motivators) they constantly reaffirm to themselves, whether they are performing the act or not.

You will find that by asking these exceptional people the right questions, you will get incredibly revealing answers that will help you apply what you see and what you hear to your own life, thereby greatly reducing the time it will take you to achieve a similar level of achievement.

For if you adopt the "act as if" idea of your *already having* the skills, actions and attitudes you want, soon you will become that which you've been acting.

| LIFE'S WORDS OF WISDOM |

There is no moment like the present.
The man who will not execute his resolutions
when they are fresh upon him
can have no hope for them afterwards:
they will be dissipated, lost and perish
in the hurry and scurry of the world,
or sunk in the slough of indolence.

—Maria Edgeworth

LESSON 87

LEARNING FROM THE "SOMEDAY I'LL," "IF ONLY I HAD" AND "I SHOULD HAVE" EXPERIENCES

For all the sad words of tongues or pen, the saddest are these: It might have been.
—John Greenleaf Whittier

The world is full of people who never believed enough in themselves to go for their dreams. You can pick them out in a crowd with ease, for these are the ones who say, "If only I would've," or "I should've done this or that."

Just as easily to pick out are the future losers. These are the people who today will say, "Someday I'll do this or that." For most of these people, their "someday I'll's" are only a pipe dream that will never be realized, because they, like the losers of the past, will not do the one thing absolutely necessary for success.

THE LESSON TO BE LEARNED IS…

The one ingredient that these well-intentioned folks didn't do and won't do is take action. For it is only action that sets the forces in motion to make your dreams and goals come true. Belief backed up with action turns your "I wish" and "I hope" into "I can" and "I will."

But simply taking action is not enough. Your action must be focused. Taking action is much like a light bulb that lights your room. It isn't very powerful or intense, but it doesn't need to be, because it's scattered all over the place.

But if you take that same scattered light and focus it into a powerful laser beam, you can burn through objects. That's the kind of power you have when you take focused action.

And to really reach your goal quickly and succeed like you've never succeeded before, you must apply massive amounts of unrelenting and unstoppable energy to that focused action.

The bombardment of focused action with massive amounts of unstoppable energy behind it is such a powerful force that even the most stubborn of obstacles is easily destroyed.

[IF I ONLY KNEW THEN WHAT I KNOW NOW™]

LESSON 88

TELL ME WHAT YOU WANT, NOT WHAT YOU DON'T

Any idea that is held in the mind that is either feared or revered will begin at once to clothe itself in the most convenient and appropriate physical forms available.
—Andrew Carnegie

By now, you know the invisible laws of success.

You should also know by now that your mind is a faithful servant and will bring you the people and experiences that are in perfect harmony with your dominant thoughts. For your subconscious mind always magnifies and multiplies those things to which you give your dominant attention, that is, the things you think about most—pleasant or unpleasant.

So what do most people focus on?

You've got it, the things that they don't want to happen in their lives. And since these are things that they think about most, what do you imagine to be the unfailing and totally predictable outcome?

Right again, they keep getting more of the same.

THE LESSON TO BE LEARNED IS…

To eliminate the unpleasantness, struggle, hurt and heartache, keep your mind only on the things you want to happen and off of the things you don't want to happen.

:: The Lessons of Life and What They're Trying to Teach You ::

As you know, your mind is like a powerful magnet that will attract the people, circumstances and conditions that relate to the thoughts you think most. If those thoughts are about having a new life, a better life or a more fulfilling life, your subconscious mind will show you how you can have it and what steps you need to take to achieve it.

When you realize this simple truth, you begin to see that life truly is fair and not out to get you and hold you down in misery, struggle and hardship. For it is when you decide to take control of the thoughts you think and what you think most about during the day that you will understand that you really do become that which you give your attention to. In life, it can be no other way.

LESSON 89

THE POWER OF WORDS

*People can have what they say.
The problem is they keep saying what they have.*
—Charles Capps

Words.

Could they be the most powerful force there is?

Many would say so, as life is filled with many a story of contrasts of how a few harsh words or words of encouragement and belief changed people's lives.

Words have the power to affect you for the rest of your life.

And though you may never realize it, the words you spoke to someone, somewhere and at some time, changed the life of someone.

You can probably recall that the same thing happened to you.

If words are so important, then how much of an effect do the things we tell ourselves every day—in the form of self-talk—pull us in the direction of those words and the beliefs behind them?

A lot.

Your mind listens to everything you tell it, even if you're just kidding.

It doesn't question whether the information is true or not.

:: The Lessons of Life and What They're Trying to Teach You ::

If you tell yourself something over and over, your mind will accept that as a command from you that this is exactly what you want to experience and happen in your life.

And you wonder why things are the way they are for so long.

THE LESSON TO BE LEARNED IS...

You cannot become and experience anything more or different than what you tell yourself.

You simply cannot rise above your words.

So the most important thing is to tell yourself whatever it is you want, but make sure those words are pure, powerful, positive, and unlimiting.

The right words—with deep conviction and belief behind them—will take you to the top faster than anything you've experienced.

The wrong words will pull you down and keep you there indefinitely, that is, until you start telling yourself the right words.

Listen to people and the words they use.

Just a few minutes of conversation with them will tell you if they're on their way to the top or moving in the direction of someplace you don't even want to go.

Yes, my friend, words are awesomely powerful, so choose your words carefully.

Your mind is listening.

LIFE'S WORDS OF WISDOM

*The greater the obstacle,
the more glory in overcoming it.*

—Moliere

LESSON 90

YOU CAN CLIMB THE HIGHEST MOUNTAIN

*Courage is the finest of human qualities
because it guarantees all the others.*
—Winston Churchill

Let me share an experience that changed my life.

It happened in Japan when I had the opportunity to climb Mt. Fuji, Japan's highest mountain.

We began our trek at 2:30 in the morning, because we wanted to climb as high as we could before daylight so we could see the sunrise. I don't how we did it, climbing so fast with backpacks, climbing sticks and flashlights, but somehow we managed to get to 10,000 feet before sunrise.

As I sat on one of the edges of the mountain, I looked out at the country below me and felt something I had never experienced before.

I was on top of the world, feeling closer than ever to my Creator and overcome by the sensation of being able to reach out and touch the heavens.

Then it happened.

The most incredible sunrise I had ever experienced. For those few incredible minutes, I was higher than the sun and it had to rise up and touch me.

As the sun began to rise, I started to climb again.

As I made my way past 10,500 feet, I was above the clouds and it began to rain upward. The wind was carrying the moisture upward and, as it did, the water poured straight up and all over my face.

What a feeling!

As I came closer to the peak, the air became thinner and thinner, and it was all I could do to walk 20 steps before having to stop to catch my breath. The height was one thing, but the steep mountain climb and the speed at which I was climbing made it that much tougher.

As the steps became progressively tougher, I began playing mind games and setting up small goals of walking 10, 15, or 20 steps. Each time I accomplished a goal, it would give me energy to accomplish my next goal, and so on.

Every time it looked like the top of the mountain was just over the next cliff, there was another cliff to greet me.

Looking down at how far I had come kept the fire burning inside me to stay focused on conquering the next cliff and then the next until finally the last cliff would be conquered.

Finally, the last cliff *was* conquered, as I made it to the top, at 12,388 feet, by 9:00 a.m.—and boy, was it cold!

I walked around and realized that I had climbed the highest mountain—at least in Japan.

But what a powerful experience it was—spiritually, emotionally, physically and, little did I realize then, for my future success.

THE LESSON TO BE LEARNED IS...

I can't even begin to tell you how many times I've thought back to the Mt. Fuji experience whenever I've been

:: The Lessons of Life and What They're Trying to Teach You ::

faced with hardship, trials and tribulations in my life.

Knowing that you've climbed the highest mountain—at least in Japan—is a powerful motivator to know that whatever you're going through now isn't nearly as tough as climbing that mountain in such a short amount of time. Those feelings of "nothing could stop me then and nothing can stop me now" are instantly replayed whenever I think about the Mt. Fuji experience.

And while you may not have had the opportunity or desire to climb a mountain like Mt. Fuji, the important lesson here is to push yourself and break the limits and do something you may have never done before.

Some people bungee jump, skydive, do whitewater rafting, explore a new country or trek through some jungle. Whatever it is you want to do, or that which you've been wanting to do, by all means do it!

You won't believe the positive way that experience will change your life for years afterward.

It's so easy to get so caught up the daily grind. We tend not to push ourselves to experience new and different things that give our minds new reference points to go back to, time and time again, to propel us to the next level of success.

If fear is holding you back, remember that you were born with only two fears: the fear of falling and the fear of loud noises. Every other fear has been learned.

The great news is that even the fear of falling and loud noises can be conquered and conquered quite easily if the desire to experience and grow is there.

Once you have the life-changing experience and exhilaration of breaking out of the comfort zone, your success and belief in yourself will grow faster than you ever imagined.

You can climb the highest mountain.

LESSON 91

IF YOU COMPARE, GET READY FOR DESPAIR

Being unhappy is easy; just compare your life to others'.

People love to compare. Be it their jobs, cars they drive, houses they own, clothes they wear, people they know, things they do, money and possessions, and experiences they have, comparison either makes them feel real good or real bad.

Too often, comparing is a feel-bad experience.

Let's change that.

THE LESSON TO BE LEARNED IS...

For a day, try living in a vacuum.

No, I don't mean a Dyson or a Hoover.

I'm talking about living in your own little world and enjoying all the blessings you have and not comparing yourself in any way to anyone on that day.

Can you do it?

It might be tougher than you think.

Yet if you can, get ready for a surprise.

You will find an inner sense of calm and peace coming over you in a way you haven't felt in a long time.

You will have realized that there's no need to beat yourself up and make yourself feel bad by all the constant comparison and judgment of others you've been doing for so long.

Remember: there's no comparison when it comes to feeling good.

:: The Lessons of Life and What They're Trying to Teach You ::

LESSON 92

YOU WERE DESIGNED TO CREATE, NOT COMPETE

There will always be someone different, but never better than you.

If you believe that no one like you ever was or ever will be created—which is the absolute truth—then why would you want to compete with anyone and want to be like them?

Competition can be one of the biggest feel-bad experiences we can have. With competition, there always has to be a winner and a loser; someone to feel good and someone to feel bad.

Competition can also be driven by the belief of lack and limitation; that there's not enough to go around for everyone, so you'd better get in, grab what you can and get the heck out. If by chance, the other person gets a few crumbs, great; and if not, that's their tough luck.

Yet it's that kind of belief that keeps so many people from ever developing their true creative potential and using their one-of-a-kind unique gifts to bless the lives of others and to give themselves the deep sense of lasting inner fulfillment and rewards in life that they can't or won't get in any other way.

THE LESSON TO BE LEARNED IS…

By competing with others, you're using their level of achievement as a benchmark for your success. And you know what? Doing so automatically gets you right in the middle of that comparison thing, and you know what happens when you compare.

Competing also means giving your sense of happiness to a variable you can't totally control.

Not that you always have total control over everything in your life; you don't.

However, you can keep every bit of the control that you do have and direct it in the ways that you do want and not to the unpredictable direction of the competitive winds.

The most successful and truly happy people compete with only one person, themselves; nothing and nobody else dictates what they do and when they do it.

They realize there's no way they can compare themselves to anyone or anything. For how can they, when they are the only one like them with their gifts, talents, abilities, dreams and desires?

Yes, my friend, right now you live in a world of incredible abundance that's filled with plenty to go around for everyone.

Develop yourself to the fullest of your abilities, use those abilities to touch the lives of others and you won't have the time or desire to compare or compete with anyone.

LIFE'S WORDS OF WISDOM

Fear not that thy life shall come to an end, but rather fear that it shall never have a beginning.

—Cardinal Newman

[IF I ONLY KNEW THEN WHAT I KNOW NOW™]

LESSON 93

SAY GOODBYE TO THE ASSASSINS OF YOUR SUCCESS AND HAPPINESS
---

*Fear knocked at the door. Faith answered.
And lo, no one was there.*

—Anonymous

What if I told you that many people right now are hiring success hit men whose sole job is to keep them from ever experiencing any kind of success in their lives?

Sounds crazy, doesn't it?

Yet, these assassins are deadlier than any Navy SEAL, Special Forces operator or anyone you will ever see in the movies, because they never miss and they never stop.

In fact, they can't get enough of this assassination stuff.

So they create more assassins to infiltrate the lives of friends, family and co-workers.

And the only things that keep them alive and going are fear, doubt and worry.

THE LESSON TO BE LEARNED IS…

When it has come to you that, when going for your dreams, living a great life and having the things you truly want, fear, doubt and worry may have stopped you more times than you realized.

The fear of the unknown and what others might say or think if you don't succeed.

The nagging doubt that's played over and over in your mind, reminding yourself, "What makes you so darn sure you're good enough, talented enough or have what it takes to do the things you're dreaming or telling yourself you want to do?"

The worry of thinking you're too old, you don't have the education or money, you don't know the right people or it's too late for you to do it, now that you have a family or relationship.

All these things have and will continue to keep you stuck in the quicksand of where you are right now until you finally realize that all fear, doubt and worry are imaginary.

That's right; they don't exist anywhere except in your mind.

So how do you get rid of them?

By re-focusing your thoughts.

Focusing on the things you want to achieve.

Seeing and feeling the result of your already having lived and achieved that which you want.

Giving yourself the positive and empowering self-talk—always verbalized in the present tense as if you have and are enjoying those qualities right now—and seeing in your mind and feeling the terrific emotions of the reasons you want to do, be and have the things that you do.

For if you have enough reasons, you will find enough ways to have whatever it is that you want.

[IF I ONLY KNEW THEN WHAT I KNOW NOW™]

LESSON 94

THE POWER OF AN ORGANIZED MIND

Let a man radically alter his thoughts, and he will be astonished at the rapid transformation it will effect in the material conditions of his life.

—James Allen

Many people complain that they just can't seem to find the time to do what they really want to do. They may even say that they're organized, yet their actions say something entirely different.

Look at their desks, homes, closets, cars, or appearance. All these are merely indicators of how well organized their internal thinking and direction is.

Surveys have found that people with organized work environments make on the average many times more than their messy counterparts.

The outside is only a reflection of the inside, and what a message it can tell!

THE LESSON TO BE LEARNED IS...

When it comes to success and achievement, why is it important for you to be organized?

Oh, that's simple.

To start with, organization eliminates guesswork; you know where things are when you need to have them. Just by doing that, you decrease anxiety and stress and empower yourself to feel more in control of your life.

All of this helps you find the time to release your creativity, which will increase your self-worth, thereby helping you want to use your gifts, talents and abilities to provide service to others, which in turn raises your market value to society, thereby increasing your wealth and giving you the rewards of a better lifestyle, a sense of accomplishment and deep fulfillment.

And I've only just begun....

LESSON 95

TIMING IS EVERYTHING

*All things happen when they're ready,
and not a moment sooner.*

Haven't you found that to be true?

How many times in your life has it happened that you planned and planned and did everything needed for success, but your timing wasn't quite right and that deal you wanted didn't happen in the time and way you thought?

It is little wonder so many people are frustrated.

THE LESSON TO BE LEARNED IS…

The reality is that people want to control everything. They want things to happen and they want them to happen when *they* want them to happen. However, whether it's romance, finance, career, fun, hobbies or whatever, there is a perfect time for anything and everything.

One of the most profound lessons successful people in life say they learned was *that their timing was off because they weren't in synch with the higher purpose for their lives.* All things happen in God's perfect timing, and everything will work in divine perfect order for your life *if you let it.*

These people have found that when your prayers, needs and desires are answered, so are many others people's answered at the same time.

:: The Lessons of Life and What They're Trying to Teach You ::

Step back for a moment and look at some of the things that have happened to you when your timing was right on.

You'll be amazed to find how making your dream come true also made the dreams of many others come true too.

That's the way it's supposed to be; each of us wanting the best for each other and doing what we can to make our lives and theirs better at the same time.

Once your timing is right, your world will be right.

LESSON 96

WHERE ARE ALL THE HEROES?

To believe in the heroic makes heroes.
—Benjamin Disraeli

We live in a world that is filled with movie stars, music stars and superstar athletes. And yet, with so many famous faces, where are all the heroes?

Since when did fame, fortune or level of outrageousness towards the general public ever become prerequisites for induction to the heroes club?

Many have asked the question, "Would we know a hero if we saw one?"

THE LESSON TO BE LEARNED IS…

Inside you right now is everything you need to become a hero—that incredible someone who can make a huge impact on the lives of others.

You might be shaking your head and thinking, "Yeah, right. Me, a hero." But it is true.

You don't need money or fame to change the world and be a hero.

Look at what Mother Teresa of Calcutta did with the poor of India and how she changed the world by her compassion.

Look at what Gandhi did with no weapons.

He changed the course of a country by his example of love and peace. His influence captivated a nation of over 200 million people who wanted to embrace what he believed.

History is filled with heroes who started off with far less than you have right now, yet believed enough in a cause greater than themselves and devoted their life to it.

These are the heroes who have stood the test of time and the ones that society remembers.

My question to you, my friend, is this: Will your life be one people remember?

[IF I ONLY KNEW THEN WHAT I KNOW NOW™]

LESSON 97

RUNNING AROUND IN CIRCLES

*Change your thoughts
and you change your world.*

—Norman Vincent Peale

Whenever you get tired, just remember you're lucky you're not a caterpillar.

The story is told of a scientist who took caterpillars and placed them in a complete circle around a flowerpot.

Then he watched.

Round and round the flowerpot they went, nonstop, for 24 hours a day.

On the third and fourth days, he put pine needles—their food—into the center of the flowerpot.

Then he watched again.

A funny thing happened.

The caterpillars—even with their food in the center of the pot they were circling—kept going round and round that flower pot for 7 full days and nights until they literally dropped dead from starvation and exhaustion—even with an abundance of food that was only inches away.

It makes you think that no person would ever do that.

And while we hope that people have enough sense to get off the merry-go-round and treadmill that leads only to life's frustrations and disappointments, many don't.

:: The Lessons of Life and What They're Trying to Teach You ::

Just like the caterpillar, they still haven't learned that if they keep doing the same things they're doing, they're bound to keep getting the same things they're getting.

THE LESSON TO BE LEARNED IS...

Look at your life right now.

Look at it over the last four years.

Has much of it has really changed?

How much money have you saved?

How much closer are you to your goals (that is, if you have them)?

If you're not getting ahead or have been getting by or merely surviving and keeping your head above water because you keep running around in circles, who in the world sold you on that plan for living your life?

Leave the running around in circles to the caterpillars.

You're going to be busy with a brand new life to live.

| LIFE'S WORDS OF WISDOM |

*I found Rome a city of bricks,
and left it a city of marble.*

—Augustus Caesar

LESSON 98

YOU MUST FIRST GIVE THAT WHICH YOU WISH TO RECEIVE

You must first pay the price for success before you receive the rewards of success.
—Anonymous

Many people believe that success in life is like eating at a restaurant; you get whatever you want first and then pay for it later.

If only it were true.

THE LESSON TO BE LEARNED IS…

Whatever you want, you can have. But first you must give it away or pre-pay for it, before it and the rewards of success will flow back to you.

Life is like a wave; what starts out as a small ripple quickly becomes bigger and bigger, until whatever you send out covers the entire lake.

And whatever it is you first give out is returned to you many times greater than the amount you originally gave out.

Test it.

Whatever you want, give first, and watch what you receive.

LIFE'S WORDS OF WISDOM

There are high spots in all of our lives. And most of them have come through the encouragement of someone else. I don't care how great, how famous or successful a man or woman may be, each hungers for applause.

—George Matthew Adams

[IF I ONLY KNEW THEN WHAT I KNOW NOW™]

LESSON 99

YOU DON'T KNOW HOW MUCH YOU AFFECT OTHER PEOPLE

Example is not the main thing influencing others. It is the only thing.

—Albert Schweitzer

I remember it well.

I was at a party and some woman I knew only fairly well, sat down with me and said, "You don't know how much you affect other people."

Hearing that for the first time was like being hit with a ton of bricks.

Wow! What an impact.

I greatly appreciated what she said, and from that day on I've made it a point to go out of my way to make time for others. Really get into their heads. Make them think. Force them to examine their lives and pull themselves up by the bootstraps.

I've met many others who have decided to make time for others too, and their reactions from people, like what I've seen in my own experiences, range from shock to real joy.

I'll bet you're one who likes to help people too.

Only a handful of people ever take the time to ask the questions of others that cause them to go beyond the "Hey, how's it going?" habitual response.

As you can imagine, if you desire to positively affect the lives of others, many of the people you encounter will want to pull away from you because you have caused those squeaky, rusty wheels in their brain to start working again.

Yet, as the great philosopher Socrates has said, "A life unexamined is a life not worth living."

THE LESSON TO BE LEARNED IS…

You may be in a regular job, with a regular family and have a regular life. Nothing, you say, that Hollywood would want to make a movie about.

But, that doesn't make any difference at all to how you can affect others.

People really don't listen to you as much as they watch you.

The old advice that actions speak louder than words is true.

The example you set by living your life the way you do will influence more people you know and don't know, than any degree you can obtain or eloquent words you may speak.

It all begins with making your life a statement—first and foremost to yourself, then to the world—that each day you live the things you believe.

Go ahead and feel proud, and do it your own way.

People are watching.

They want to be inspired.

LESSON 100

YOUR WORD IS YOUR BOND

If your word's no good, you're no good.
—Adam Wolff

My father was never a rich man.

Yet he was a good man, a hard-working man, a serious man who loved the outdoors, loved doing things for other people and lived by the belief that if your word's no good, you're no good.

"After all," he used to say, "what does a person have in their life except their reputation that is built from their word backed by action."

Many people have experience after experience of disappointment, all because they took someone at their word.

Maybe you have too.

It can shake the very foundations of your belief in the good of others, can't it?

Today, there seems to be a nonchalant, "Who gives a care?" type of attitude emanating from so many people who say the things you want to hear, yet won't do the things they tell you they will, when they say they'll do them.

But that's good news for those who do.

THE LESSON TO BE LEARNED IS…

One of the greatest things you will ever do is develop honor and character. For those are the things that no one can take away and that will stay with you for the rest of your life.

So how do you do that?

Easy.

Just remember this:

If you sow an Action, you'll reap a Habit.

If you sow a Habit, you'll reap a Character.

If you sow a Character, you'll reap a Destiny.

After you are gone from this earth, the one thing people will remember about you is what kind of person you were.

Were you a person of your word?

A person of honor?

A person of integrity?

A person whose word was your living bond, so that if you told someone you would do something or become something, "they could take your word to the bank," because come heck or high water, you would do it?

In this world, the doors of opportunity and success will fly wide open for you today if you are a person of your word, because the world is just full of those who are not.

Just being a person of your word is enough to propel you past the majority of others out there, those who want to do the same things you are doing, yet never will, because they'll say what they'll do, but rarely will they do what they say.

LIFE'S WORDS OF WISDOM

All dream, but not all equally. Those who dream by night in the dusty recesses of their minds wake in the day to find it was vanity; but the dreamers of the day are dangerous, for they may act their dreams with open eyes, to make it possible.

—Lawrence of Arabia

LESSON 101

THE COURAGE TO STAND ALONE

It is a rough road that leads to the heights of greatness.
—Lucius Annaeus Seneca

The road to becoming who you are meant to be is the greatest road you will ever travel.

But be prepared, for along the way, it can get very lonely after you've broken away from the crowd.

Yet, there is something inside you that, once you've decided to follow this road, will always give you the courage to weather any storm and stand alone, for however long that may be.

THE LESSON TO BE LEARNED IS...

While you travel along your life's road, many times you'll wonder if you're doing the right thing. Yet, something inside says "Yes, just keep going."

The more you learn about yourself and improve yourself, the less you may find you have in common with those happy-go-lucky friends and people you used to enjoy spending time with.

You begin to ask yourself if there's something wrong with you, since the more you thirst and learn about how to make yourself and your life the miracle it is meant to be, the less you feel drawn into living your old kind of lifestyle.

And if you're a single person who's been looking for that special person to share your life with, be patient, for as you do more work on improving yourself, your available pool of potential mates decreases.

But that's okay, because those who remain are those who are the exceptional people who are good for you and with whom you will share a powerful bond.

They are, like you, among those who won't accept anything or anyone less than someone who can inspire them to greatness and who has the potential and desire to help you grow (and you for them) in ways neither of you dreamed possible.

The world has always at first considered as outcasts, those who had the courage to stand alone. Then, as these people achieved, accomplished and became the exceptional people they were designed to be, the world embraced them, loved them, looked up to them and learned from them.

Stand tall and be proud.

You are one of them.

[IF I ONLY KNEW THEN WHAT I KNOW NOW™]

LESSON 102

THE POWER OF DISCIPLINE

Just one disciplined action will bring you many rewards.

—Jim Rohn

How many times have you heard the word *discipline*? Many people still think it's something you do to correct someone else's behavior. And because they've grown up past the disciplining years, they believe discipline doesn't apply to them anymore.

Yet, they're missing the real meaning of discipline and how once applied, it will change any area of their lives.

Discipline just isn't for kids.

THE LESSON TO BE LEARNED IS...

To accomplish anything in life, you must first take action. For if you never start, it's absolutely certain you won't arrive.

And if action is the prerequisite to success, discipline is the engine that puts action into gear.

The more disciplined you are, the more you will accomplish and the faster you will accomplish it.

Yet being disciplined not only helps accomplish your goal, it also brings you many other rewards just by doing that one disciplined action.

Let me explain.

:: The Lessons of Life and What They're Trying to Teach You ::

Let's say that you want to lose 10 pounds of fat—not weight, but fat, because there is a huge difference between the two.

So you take one disciplined action of doing just one thing: eating healthier foods.

Yet look at what happens just by your doing that one disciplined action:

1. Your body now has more energy because of the healthy foods you are eating.

2. You feel better and not so sluggish.

3. Your digestion has improved.

4. You sleep better.

5. Your skin complexion has improved.

6. You're saving money because, on average, it costs you less to eat healthy foods than processed and junk foods.

7. You're getting leaner each week—losing the fat and keeping your lean muscle tissue—because you're now eating the proper ratio of protein, carbohydrates and fat.

8. And because you're feeling and looking better, your appearance is improving, thereby raising your self-confidence, self-image and self-esteem.

9. All of this helps improve your relationships with others, your job performance and your belief in yourself that you can set goals and achieve them.

10. And because you see and feel the results from just doing one disciplined action of eating healthier, you now have a strong desire to begin an exercise program, which will change your body and the way you feel, even quicker. And it will give you even more rewards.

Take a good look at that.

Ten benefits and rewards just by taking one disciplined action.

And you can experience the same number or rewards—and probably a lot more—by being disciplined in every area of your life.

It seems that life has an unwritten creed: "The harder you are on yourself [the more disciplined you are], the easier life will be. Whereas the easier you are on yourself [the less disciplined you are], the harder life will be."

The choice has always been yours.

Choose discipline and get ready for all the rewards.

LESSON 103

THE LAST IMPRESSION

The reason most people do not like to hear the story of your troubles is that they have a big flock of their own.
—Anonymous

Think for a moment about the last conversation or meeting you had with a friend, lover, co-worker or family member.

How was it?

Positive or negative?

Happy or unhappy?

Exciting or boring?

How you answer will determine the attitude you'll start with the next time you meet that person.

Your mind tends to remember your last encounter as the last impression it associates with that person or event. If you had a great time with them or doing something together, your mind naturally looks forward to seeing them or doing that event again.

Conversely, if the experience wasn't so happy, your mind will think of ways for you to avoid that person, delay them and come up with excuses why you may not want to experience the same thing again.

THE LESSON TO BE LEARNED IS…

The last words spoken or the actions and experiences you had with someone, are the ones they remember when you're gone, so always leave a great last impression.

Many people wonder why others won't return their calls or want to avoid them. Yet if these same people will stop for a moment and take a good look at their words, attitudes and actions, they will find that they are the ones who are turning other people off and closing the doors to friendships, opportunities and happiness.

Always be aware of the last impression you want to leave with somebody.

They'll remember it long after you're gone.

| LIFE'S WORDS OF WISDOM |

*When you choose not to dream today,
you've given up your chance to live the life of
what those dreams could be tomorrow.*

[IF I ONLY KNEW THEN WHAT I KNOW NOW™]

LESSON 104

IT'S WHAT YOU DO THAT DETERMINES THE KIND OF LIFE YOU'LL LIVE

The world is blessed most by men who do things, and not by those who merely talk about them.
—James Oliver

I've got a few questions for you.

What is it that has you turned on? I mean, what has you getting up early, hitting it hard all day with passion and enthusiasm and staying up late because you absolutely love what you're doing?

If you can't answer that, then go ahead give me one good reason why.

Some people want to believe that if they really wanted to do something, they could do it and be successful.

Yet, these same people keep telling themselves this same old song and dance, year after year, as their precious life ticks by, until one day, their life is over and the clock simply ran out of time.

THE LESSON TO BE LEARNED IS...

When it comes to becoming who you want, doing what you want and having the life you want, the only thing that matters is what you *do*.

It's not about what you *can* do.

If you have enough reasons to do something, you will find plenty of ways to do it and achieve it.

:: The Lessons of Life and What They're Trying to Teach You ::

You see, my friend, when you fail to dream today, you've given up your chance to live the life of what those dreams could be tomorrow.

And when you make *no* decision (like so many people), you have chosen not to decide.

Having great *potential* to do something and not *doing* it is just like being a person who *doesn't* read and being no better than the person who *can't*.

Forget about dwelling on all your great potential and ability.

Of course you've got it; tremendous amounts of it you're not even aware of.

Focus your thoughts, images, words and energies on doing, doing, doing.

[IF I ONLY KNEW THEN WHAT I KNOW NOW™]

LESSON 105

BECOME A SEEKER OF TRUTH

No man may become an accurate thinker until he learns to separate mere gossip and information from facts.
—Napoleon Hill

The greatest teachers, sages, philosophers and other people have one thing in common: All of them are seekers of truth.

They think their own thoughts and listen with an open mind to the thoughts, ideas and beliefs of others; yet they question everything they hear and read and make a wise decision based on fact and not gossip.

Many times in life, people will make statements to others, in the hopes that these unquestioning people will accept what is told to them as the truth.

A lot of people do. Yet, it is the wise man and woman who listens to all the verbiage and then asks the person making the statement, "What basis of fact do you have for what you've told me?"

Get ready and listen to the silence.

THE LESSON TO BE LEARNED IS...

You'll find that many people love to simply repeat what they've read or heard—and even make it up—to sway you to their side of thinking and have you see them as an authority or someone in the know.

Many do all the talking as a front for a weak self-image. The wise course of action is for you to question everything.

Most people won't question what they hear, for fear of upsetting or disrespecting the other person.

There also seems to be a great fear in many people to question the religious beliefs that were instilled in them as a child.

When you look at the life of Jesus, you see He was a seeker of truth and quite a rebel. Yet, does that make His message any less powerful, meaningful and life changing? Of course not.

By failing to question what you see, hear and read, you show more disrespect to yourself by not giving yourself all the facts—as many as you possibly can—about the things that are important to your life. Those facts will help you make wise decisions.

What you hear and read and accept as truth are the beliefs that make up much of how you see people, life, your life, your ability and your success and, eventually, the happiness you allow yourself to experience.

Truth always prevails and stands the test of time.

Most of the ideas and opinions of people are as fleeting and changeable as the wind. Listening to and accepting the ideas and beliefs of others, without questioning them or seeking the truth, is like building your house on a foundation of sand that can quickly be destroyed by the storms of life.

However, being a seeker of truth is like building that same house on solid rock; always able to withstand the storms of life, however often and severe they may be.

Learn from the greatest humans who have ever and will ever walk the face of this earth.

Always let truth be your guide.

LESSON 106

LIFE IS EXPERIENCE

Experience is the name everyone gives to their mistakes.

—Oscar Wilde

Experiences are the lessons for us to learn in the University of Life.

The more experiences we have, the more we learn and the faster we can grow.

Your life is exciting in proportion to the number of things you have to look forward to. And you create those things to look forward to when you have lots of projects you're involved with, lots of goals you want to achieve, and by keeping yourself open and desiring to experience new things each day.

THE LESSON TO BE LEARNED IS...

Many people don't want new experiences for fear of the unknown. They seem to live by the motto, "I'd rather not know what I'm missing and be bored than experience something new and grow."

What these people don't realize is that life will allow them to stagnate for only so long before the experiences they've put off are placed in their path so they will be forced to grow.

The key to getting the most out of each day and the experience it brings is to be happy with what you have while you are going after what you want.

Many people want to defer their happiness until they finally have enough money, get their dream home, go on their dream vacation, raise the kids, or any of a host of other excuses.

But it's trap, because those things are never over with; there's always something else to take their place.

Make all you can out of everything you have right now.

Use what you have to create and enjoy the experiences you want.

Welcome *all* experiences. You never know which will be the magic one that can turn around your thinking, belief, attitude and life.

Tear down your self-erected walls so you can live a life of experiencing, learning, living and loving.

Learn. Change. Grow. Become!

:: The Lessons of Life and What They're Trying to Teach You ::

LESSON 107

EXPERIENCE HAS NOTHING TO DO WITH ABILITY

Nothing in the world can take place of persistence. Talent will not; nothing is more common than unsuccessful men with talent. Genius will not; unrewarded genius is almost a proverb. Education will not; the world is full of educated derelicts. Persistence and determination alone are omnipotent. The slogan 'Press On' has solved and always will solve the problems of the human race.

—Calvin Coolidge

Lets' talk for a moment about a kind of experience that keeps more people from going for their dreams and more employers from hiring them.

It's called experience, and it has absolutely nothing to do with ability.

Society would like you to believe that the only sure route to real success in life is to have a college degree.

Hardly.

The only thing you can be absolutely certain of when you get a college degree is that you have a college degree.

That degree is no entrée and guarantee that you'll be hired and successful.

Where did the belief come from that unless you have the experience in doing something you certainly won't have the ability to do it or do it well?

It reminds me of the story of the young girl who wanted to study music and become a famous pianist. One day she went to see one of the most famous music teachers in the world.

As the young girl sat down, the maestro entered the room and quickly glanced at her and spoke, "What is that you want? I'm very busy and have little time for chit chat."

The girl said she wanted to study music. The old curmudgeon looked at her and with a sneer said, "Can you play the piano?" The girl, unfazed by his tirade, quietly spoke, "I don't know, sir; I never tried."

Turns out she had the desire and natural talent to become one of the greatest the world has known.

The point is, she didn't have the experience, but she had the ability.

The master saw that inside her was a desire, backed with ability that was far more important than any experience she had.

THE LESSON TO BE LEARNED IS…

Right now, there patiently waits inside you the *ability* to make your deepest desires and dreams come true, without your ever having had the previous experience to do so. For if you have the desire to do something, you also come with the ability to make that desire happen.

Desire and ability always go together.

It's time to answer that quiet voice and deep ache inside you from all the years of not following your desires and not going for your dreams just because you've been holding on to the belief that you don't have the experience.

:: The Lessons of Life and What They're Trying to Teach You ::

Take one small step in the direction of that which you most desire.

Just one small step. That's all.

Then tomorrow, take another small step.

You don't need big steps or radical changes to your life to become great or happy and to make your dreams come true.

Small steps will do it.

[IF I ONLY KNEW THEN WHAT I KNOW NOW™]

LESSON 108

YOUR ACTIONS SAY WHO AND WHAT YOU ARE AND WHAT YOU BELIEVE

*What you do speaks so loud
that I cannot hear what you say.*
—Ralph Waldo Emerson

From the words you speak to the clothes you wear, your actions say it all.

Your outside world mirrors what you believe on the inside.

It's been said that people will treat you the way you teach them to treat you, and the way you teach them is by the words you speak and the actions you do.

For years, people go through life frustrated and cynical at other people because they listen to what others say and don't observe what they do. The light turns on for these folks when they finally realize that the only thing that truly matters is what someone will do, not what they'll say they'll do.

THE LESSON TO BE LEARNED IS…

People have an uncanny way of telling you what you want to hear, when you want to hear it.

This happens all the time in relationships and business. You want to believe the words, because they sound just so darned good.

But, people are people, and many times they can't do what they say. In those cases, you need to make allowances and give them your understanding.

However, when it comes to those who chronically feed you bull, who tell you things that are probably too good to be true, they are the ones to, as they say in England, "measure twice and cut once" with.

You'll save yourself a lot of wasted time, emotions, money and heartache if you'll observe only what they do and not just listen to what they say.

| LIFE'S WORDS OF WISDOM |

No man ever became great or good except through many and great mistakes.

—William E. Gladstone

[IF I ONLY KNEW THEN WHAT I KNOW NOW™]

LESSON 109

I AM RESPONSIBLE

To find the real causes of your mistakes, simply do one thing; stand in front of the mirror.

What I'm about to tell you are the three most important words you can say for anything that has happened, is happening or will happen to you in your life.

They are also the hardest.

"I am responsible."

Admit it. We don't like to be held accountable for the things that happen in our lives if we can help it. So people do what people have always done: make up excuses and blame others, bad luck or any other thing for why something doesn't work out or hasn't happened.

Yet doing that lets us off the hook, keeps us unaccountable for our actions and inactions and keeps us from becoming the architects of our lives and having the maturity to understand and direct it as we wish.

THE LESSON TO BE LEARNED IS...

When things go well, you are responsible; and when things go wrong you're also responsible. The responsibility for the welfare of your life was placed upon your shoulders when you became an adult.

Even though their age says differently, many people haven't yet become adults, because they keep blaming life and other people for their misery, lack, limitation and unhappiness. Hey, it can be hard to let go of a good thing when you think it takes the pressure off of you.

You know by now that your thoughts are things; that is, the thoughts you think tend to clothe themselves in their physical realities. Yes, creating the conditions of your life.

In the past, when things may have seemed to go wrong, if you think long and hard about it, you'll find that your thinking at that time was responsible for giving you the beliefs that allowed you to experience and accept those things in your life. Eventually, you changed your thinking and, amazingly, you changed the direction of your life.

Regardless of the excuses or thinking that you can continue to get by in life by not taking responsibility for what does or doesn't happen to you, the fact is, sooner or later, all roads will lead back to you, my friend. *You* will be held accountable.

Are you ready for that?

Of course you are.

You always have been.

It's just that up until this point, your thoughts and beliefs have allowed you to stay where you are and not go any further.

Take responsibility for everything that happens to you, and you will experience a freedom and happiness like you've never known before.

LIFE'S WORDS OF WISDOM

Bad habits are like a nice hammock; easy to get into and tough to get out of.

—Anonymous

[IF I ONLY KNEW THEN WHAT I KNOW NOW™]

LESSON 110

THE HABIT OF SUCCESS

Our self-image and our habits tend to go together. Change one and you automatically change the other.
—Dr. Maxwell Maltz

Habits are so easy to get into and so hard to get out of. Habits can propel you to the top or pull you down to the bottom of a sea of misery and keep you there.

People wonder how in the world they have the habits they do. In all honesty, they can't ever remember choosing to do the things they do. Yet, they have the habit and, for most, it only gets stronger day after day.

THE LESSON TO BE LEARNED IS…

Habits are the engines that help propel your actions.

I want you to ask yourself: "Do the habits I have make me feel good or bad?"

If you're feeling a bit down, here's a great way to change that.

It's called the 21-Day Solution, and it works like clockwork.

You see, many people have found that it takes about 21 days to create and have your subconscious mind accept a new habit. That is, you do the same thing over and over for 21 days in a row, and your mind automatically accepts that as a command from you that this is a new behavior you want to have.

Through the power of replacement, you can replace a bad habit with a good one simply by substituting the good behavior in the place of the behavior you want to be rid of. One comes in and the other goes out.

It's the tried-and-true habit of success you can use anywhere at anytime.

Just give yourself 21 days to do it.

LESSON 111

MAKE SURE TO BREAK FAST

If you could only let go of your troubles as easily as you're able to forget your blessings, what a different life you would live.

When it comes to *break fast*, I'm not talking about the first meal of the morning.

I'm talking about the pain and heartache many people continue to feel daily from not letting go of the past memories and the present frustrations of an unpleasant personal or business relationship.

Many times in life, the most effective and painless way to deal with unpleasantness in business or personal relationships is by breaking clean and fast and not looking back.

When things drag on, as most people let them, the wound tends to grow deeper and never heal. However, a clean break allows both parties to move on and thereby allows the healing to begin immediately.

THE LESSON TO BE LEARNED IS...

What relationships in your life have been causing you far too much pain for much too long?

Okay, now; of these relationships, why have you continued to remain in the relationship and continue to keep taking all the frustration you've been taking?

(Are you coming up with some good answers?)

Of these relationships, which ones are important for you to stay in, and why?

Which ones are not important for you to stay in?

Your answers will tell you the reasons for your need to stay in the relationship or that it's time to get out of it.

For all the things no longer important or working in your life, ask yourself if it's time to remove the heavy weight of emotions you've been carrying around for so long.

You may find it's the right time for break fast.

LESSON 112

GIVE EVERYTHING YOUR BEST

He did it with all his heart, and prospered.
—2 Chronicles 31:21

When was the last time you had the feeling that you really pushed yourself beyond what you normally do and gave whatever project you were involved with, your absolute very best?

If the answer was "I don't remember," we've got some serious talking to do.

Many people will push themselves and give their absolute best only when they are pushed, prodded, coerced, enticed or threatened by some outside force.

So why won't they do it because they want to?

The greatest rewards in life always go to those who give whatever they do their very best.

THE LESSON TO BE LEARNED IS...

The infection of unhappiness begins when you do less than you're capable of.

Giving whatever you do your very best makes you grow, learn, use and expand the greatness that lies within you.

The more you give of yourself, the more you will have to give, as life always overfills the cup of talents to those whose talents are used to the fullest of their abilities.

Isn't it about time your cup overflowed?

LESSON 113

YOU GROW ON THE JOURNEY

The journey of a thousand miles begins with one step.
—Lao-Tse

A lot of folks have this goal-setting-and-achieving thing all mixed up.

They mistakenly believe that achieving the result is where the happiness is found.

What they don't realize is that true success and happiness are found during the journey and never at a destination.

THE LESSON TO BE LEARNED IS...

Sure, goal setting and achieving help you to achieve something, but the far greater benefit to you is what you become on the road you take to reach your destination. For it is along each goal's road that you're taught lessons about life and yourself that you never would have learned any other way.

Set the kind of goals that will make something of you if you achieve them.

Ask yourself, "If I set this goal, what will it make of me to achieve it?" Along with that, ask yourself the following questions:

What do I want to do?

What do I want to see?

What do I want to be?

What do I want to have?

Where do I want to go?

What do I want to share?

From your beliefs to your attitudes to your actions, the goals you set will affect you all day long.

Make your goals big, and use small steps to achieve them.

Each small step has its own unique road you will journey on to learn the lessons you need to learn so you can move to the next road of success.

You're going to be amazed at what you'll become along the way.

LESSON 114

GET FOCUSED LIKE A LASER BEAM

What this power is, I cannot say. All I know is that it exists... and it becomes available only when you are in a state of mind in which you know exactly what you want... and are fully determined not to quit until you get it.
—Alexander Graham Bell

Earlier in the book, we talked about the differences between a light bulb and a laser beam. Both are sources of light, yet both are very different in what they can do.

A light bulb can illuminate a room and, because its light energy is scattered all over the place, it does it well.

A laser beam, on the other hand, is more powerful than any lightbulb could ever hope to be.

For the laser beam is concentrated light energy that is precisely focused. All of that energy, focus and precision allows that laser beam to cut through paper, wood, glass or steel.

If you want to be successful, you need to become like that laser beam.

THE LESSON TO BE LEARNED IS...

I want you to think back to a time that you wanted something, for example, a new car.

Before you decided on what kind of car you wanted, you could drive around each day and pass many of those same kinds of cars, but you didn't notice them because you didn't give your mind a clear target, picture and goal of the kind of new car you wanted.

However, once you did and told your mind—by your constant thoughts each day of thinking this is the kind of car you wanted—isn't it amazing how many of them you began to notice?

What you did was give your brain a task to achieve; and because you gave it a clear picture and command, it began making you aware of things in your daily life that matched that picture and command.

In essence, you were giving it the message "I want this," and your brain answered you back, "Okay, here it is."

Think of it as a type of radar in your brain that always has its eyes and ears open to anything that matches your most dominant thoughts, dreams, goals and desires.

When you get focused like a laser beam on deciding exactly what you want, you kick your brain into high gear and it brings you to the people, places, things and events that will help you achieve your goals. And it will do so with perfect timing.

That's why it's important for you to be crystal clear on whatever it is you want to have, be or do.

If you're unclear of why you want something, you'll only put a halfhearted effort into achieving it, and your brain will not work at its full capacity.

When you have enough reasons you want to achieve anything in life, you can achieve it; and that three pound marvel inside your head called your brain will show you how.

LIFE'S WORDS OF WISDOM

How far you go in life depends on your being tender with the young, compassionate with the aged, sympathetic with the striving, and tolerant of the weak and strong. Because someday in life you will have been all of these.

—George Washington Carver

[IF I ONLY KNEW THEN WHAT I KNOW NOW™]

LESSON 115

WELCOME TO THE UNIVERSITY OF LIFE

Each day is a gift, a learning experience meant to teach you lessons about yourself and those around you.

Every day, whether they realize it or not, people all over the world are enrolled in school.

It's called the University of Life.

But this is a different kind of school.

It's a place where one's lessons are never over and the classroom doors never close.

THE LESSON TO BE LEARNED IS...

Each day, we are taught new things about ourselves, other people, and the world we live in.

The lessons never stop, and they will keep repeating in your life until you learn from them. Once you have learned, you graduate to the next level of awareness and understanding.

For one of the lessons that the University of Life teaches is that we grow by two experiences: the joy from winning and the pain from losing.

And while many people work hard on their jobs, the University of Life demands that they work equally hard on themselves so they will achieve their goals and dreams.

For one of the lessons to be learned is that your ability will grow to match your strongest dreams.

The University of Life also wants you to understand the story of the oil well.

Vast quantities of oil are always found buried and deep within the ground. It's only when we drill for oil and bring it to the surface to be used by people, that the owner of the oil is made rich.

You are just like the oil well.

For the more you believe in yourself, in your incredible one-of-a-kind gifts, talents and abilities, and the more you have faith in the great power that guides your life, the deeper you will drill.

When you use your gifts, talents and abilities to inspire and help the lives of other people, you bring the oil from your well to the surface and you are showered with great success, wealth and the most valuable of all commodities, love and happiness.

You are truly unlimited in what you can accomplish.

For if you don't have whatever you truly want, you will either have to change your wants or change yourself. The choice is yours, and the University of Life asks you to decide.

Once you do, it's time to go drilling.

LESSON 116

ASK FOR WHAT YOU WANT

You have not, because you ask not.
—James 4:2

The world is full of abundance, with more riches for everyone than they can imagine.

Yet, most people believe in scarcity, lack and limitation.

Why?

Could it be they've never really tasted the abundance that waits for them if only they'll go for their dreams and grab it?

Many people believe they have to become something different from themselves to have what they want.

That can be an uncomfortable thought. Change always is, until it causes more pain to keep going through what you're going through than to change.

A more appropriate question may be to ask yourself, "What kind of person will I have to become to get what I want?"

Chances are all you've got to become is the person who uses their talents to bless the lives of others.

THE LESSON TO BE LEARNED IS…

We live in a world of oceans of abundance and riches.

So why is it that so many people keep going to their ocean of abundance with only a teaspoon?

:: The Lessons of Life and What They're Trying to Teach You ::

Why do people settle for so little when they can have so much?

The reason we don't have is because we don't ask; and when we do ask, it's usually for too little.

People will give you whatever you want, if only you will ask them.

You have absolutely nothing to lose by asking, for if the other person can't give you want you're asking for at that time, someone else can.

And besides, even if you get a no from one person, you haven't lost anything because they never gave you anything to lose in the first place.

So go for what you want and ask, ask, ask. After all, you have nothing to lose.

[IF I ONLY KNEW THEN WHAT I KNOW NOW™]

LESSON 117

STOP MAJORING IN MINOR THINGS

Nothing in the affairs of men is worth worrying about.
—Plato

I can't even begin to tell you how many people let the silliest, petty little things get them upset and ruin their day.

Much of their upset comes from feeling out of control of their life and the direction it's going. It's as if they've allowed themselves to become some kind of victim.

THE LESSON TO BE LEARNED IS…

You are in control of your life.

You always have been and always will be.

Can you accept that?

You bet you can.

For everything is inside you right now to make your life everything you ever dreamed of and wanted.

It's time for a little perspective.

On the grand scale of life, the things that upset you today won't even matter 50 years from now.

Change your major to the good stuff and you won't need to minor in anything to enjoy what this life has to offer.

LESSON 118

USE THE POWER OF REPLACEMENT

Once you get started you're half finished.
—Anonymous

For many people, just getting started is the toughest thing to do.

After all the analysis paralysis, taking action and actually doing something can seem like a monumental occasion. But once they do and the momentum begins, life starts getting easier and easier.

THE LESSON TO BE LEARNED IS...

Have you ever known anyone who has been away from school for some time and then decides to go back?

At first, the task seems daunting and even a bit scary. Yet, once they take action and finally do it and get into the swing of things, the fear goes away and the thirst for knowledge and learning only grows stronger.

And wouldn't you know it, that once you get in the groove of learning and accomplishing, you want to keep the momentum going. You also find that it's easy to replace one assignment with another and then another, until you become a success-achieving machine.

The same life-success principle is true for anything you do, even if you don't go to school.

The key is to immediately substitute another project for the one you just finished. Keep the momentum of success going.

Sure, you can take a break, get away for a while and enjoy what you've achieved. But once you get back, immediately start on the next project you want to accomplish.

Keep doing that for one year and you'll be amazed at how much you've achieved in such a short period of time.

Momentum is what does it.

For an object in motion is extremely difficult to stop.

You've got tremendous energy—the energy of accomplishment—behind you, and that kind of energy is incredibly powerful.

LIFE'S WORDS OF WISDOM

When things go wrong as they sometimes will,
When the road you're trudging seems all uphill,
When the funds are low and the debts are high,
And you want to smile, but you have to sigh,
When care is pressing you down a bit,
Rest if you must, but don't you quit.
Life is queer with its twists and turns,
As every one of us sometime learns,
And many a failure turns about,
When he might have won had he stuck it out.
Don't give up though the pace seems slow,
You may succeed with another blow!
Success is failure turned inside out,
The silver tint of the clouds of doubt,
And you can never tell just how close you are,
It may be near when it seems so far.
So stick to the fight when you're hardest hit,
It's when things seem worst that
you must not quit.

—Anonymous

LESSON 119

LIFE IS LIKE A WAVE

The lowest ebb is the turn of the tide.
—Henry Wadsworth Longfellow

When was the last time you watched the ocean?

I count myself blessed to live so close to the ocean, for the lessons I've learned from it have been tremendous.

Let me give you one of them.

It's called the wave, and once you understand it, life really begins to make sense.

THE LESSON TO BE LEARNED IS…

When think about it, the ocean basically does one thing; it comes in and it goes out and it does that every second of every minute, 24 hours a day.

Now the lesson of the wave is this: Great things and abundance pour into your life in a wave; and when the wave goes back out, that's the time to just be patient, maintain what you have, and wait for the next wave to come back to you.

The wave will bring you countless blessings, prosperity and abundance, and it will do so on a regular basis. Yet, the wave asks that you preserve and conserve what you have until the next wave it will bring you comes in.

And you can be absolutely assured that that next wave will come in, and come in soon.

:: The Lessons of Life and What They're Trying to Teach You ::

You need only be patient and thankful for the wave you've already received.

For the more grateful you are for what you have and the more you count yourself as blessed, the more you will be blessed.

The wave will make sure of it.

[IF I ONLY KNEW THEN WHAT I KNOW NOW™]

LESSON 120

YEARN TO LEARN

Your yearning power is much more important than your earning power.

—Anonymous

Yearning.

It's that deep desire to have, be or do something different from what you're experiencing right now.

Yearning helps you to always grow beyond that which you already are.

The more you believe in yourself and the uniqueness of your life and abilities, the more you yearn to expand your possibilities for experiencing, understanding and enjoying the things that life has to give you.

THE LESSON TO BE LEARNED IS…

When it comes to yearning and growing, you learn what you want to learn, in the amount you want to learn, when you are ready to learn it.

As you read, study and improve yourself, you'll find that the rewards are way out of proportion to the minimal amount of time you devote to doing it.

Many people place a premium on, and define success in terms of, their careers and how much they earn.

:: The Lessons of Life and What They're Trying to Teach You ::

If that's your criterion too, remember that the more you yearn, the more you learn, the more you apply, the richer you become.

To grow, you must yearn to grow.

This is the lesson life asks you to learn.

[IF I ONLY KNEW THEN WHAT I KNOW NOW™]

LESSON 121

KNOW THE DIFFERENCE BETWEEN YOU AND YOUR BODY

The way you look is not who you are.

Many years ago, I was editor of the number-one fitness publication in the world.

I count myself as blessed to have met many great people and learn from some of the greatest minds in health and fitness.

I also count myself blessed that I quickly learned how many people think of their body and who they are as one and the same.

Nothing could be further from the truth.

THE LESSON TO BE LEARNED IS...

In traveling all over the world, I have seen how men and women have let food and exercise rule their lives to the exclusion of developing themselves mentally and spiritually. Little wonder they are still crying out for balance in their lives.

For these people, their body image is their self-image.

If they look good in the mirror that day, they feel good. If not, then watch out.

Yet, how they look is simply their perception controlled by their thoughts and no one else's.

But what pain and suffering it causes them!

Your body was designed to do but one thing: carry your mind, more specifically, your brain.

Your body can't think. It merely responds to the commands given to it from your conscious and subconscious mind.

For you to look and feel the way you do, you had to first give your body a set of instructions on what it needs to do to make you feel and look a certain way.

From the foods you eat to how much sleep and exercise you do, your body merely responds to what you keep telling yourself you're supposed to do.

Sure, looking healthy and being in shape helps you feel great and gives you more energy and power. But reading more into it beyond that can be a real cause for unhappiness.

For example, your self-image and who you are as a person should not be dictated by how much muscle or fat you have or how lean or aerobically fit you are. These things are only *effects* of your beliefs and actions and not the causes, unless you allow them to be.

Your body can look and feel any way you want it to.

Sure, genetic predisposition won't allow a different body type, but it will allow you to change the body you have and make as incredible as you want within your genetic limits.

Take the time to develop all areas of that someone called "you," for you are equally physical, mental and spiritual, with the spiritual being the most powerful and life changing of them all.

Allow yourself to accept this truth: You don't need hours upon hours of aerobics and weight training to look and feel fantastic.

Anything beyond that is garbage you've allowed yourself to believe for the lies about yourself you've been willing to accept.

You are not your body; it's merely an extension of what you believe.

LIFE'S WORDS OF WISDOM

Congratulate yourself when you reach that degree of wisdom which prompts you to see less of the weaknesses of others and more of your own.

—Anonymous

[IF I ONLY KNEW THEN WHAT I KNOW NOW™]

LESSON 122

QUESTIONS CAN CHANGE YOUR LIFE

Nothing in this world is so powerful as an idea whose time has come.
—Victor Hugo

As people get older, they have a way of asking questions that is quite different from what they asked when they were children.

Instead of asking, as a child would, how this or that works and how they can do something, adults tend to ask why things happen to them.

It's that victim mindset.

Yet questions can change our lives in a hurry.

The better the question, the better the answer.

For within the deep recesses of your mind lies a power—connected to an infinite intelligence, which many call God—that knows the answer for every question you have about your life and the next step you need to take for every part of it.

Think back for a moment to any time that you were perplexed and you wondered why something was happening to you.

Chances are, you asked yourself deep and serious questions and, within a short time, you were given the answers and everything made sense.

The light turned on inside and you realized, "Wow, why didn't I see that when I was involved with that person or going through those things?"

THE LESSON TO BE LEARNED IS...

The most successful people use questions for guidance for all their future goals and dreams, and so should you.

For anything you do, always spend some quiet time away from the noise and distraction and ask yourself, "What would be the wisest course of action for me take on this matter?" Then forget you asked the question and let the answer come to you unhurriedly and in divine perfect order.

Always keep in mind that the more specific your question, the more information you will receive—information you must have to make the wisest decision possible.

[IF I ONLY KNEW THEN WHAT I KNOW NOW™]

LESSON 123

THE HIDDEN AGENDA

If the focus of your life is concentrated on getting something or going somewhere, for the rest of your life you will be on a never-ending treadmill. It's wise, from time to time, to ask yourself if it's the right treadmill and the one that's bringing you the greatest joy and happiness.

The world is full of people who have a hidden agenda.

Everybody wants something and if that want is strong enough, they will "use" people to get it.

Here's an example of what I mean; see if you can relate to it.

When I was a magazine editor, many people went out of their way to call me, write me and see me, all in the hopes of seeing what I could do for them. To help them get what they wanted.

At first, I just thought they were being nice and friendly and truly cared about what was going on with my life, but I soon found out differently.

But they were the users. These were people whose "caring performances" were Oscar-worthy. Those "I want to be your good buddy who calls you, invites you out, and really shows an interest in you and your work" people are not always what they may first appear.

For once they get what they want, they forget about you and move on to the next thing they want from someone else. Their whole lives are lived moving from one person to another in order to fulfill their hidden agenda.

THE LESSON TO BE LEARNED IS...

Just because you want things from other people doesn't mean you should lumped into the same category as the users.

The difference lies in what you give in return for the help that others give you.

Most people in life have worked hard to get where they are and achieve what they have. Chances are, they struggled through tough times way before the good times came knocking on their door.

It would be unreasonable and selfish of you to think you're the only person they have time for. So, why not give something that will benefit these people first, before ever asking for anything for yourself?

What you'll find is that those who can make a difference and help change your life in a big way and do it quickly, will be more than happy to help you. For these people are just like you. They want to help others, but they'd like to be helped too.

Don't be at all envious of the users who seem to keep climbing the ladder of success while you keep looking up at them.

Life has a wonderful way of equalizing things.

So be nice.

After the users quickly run out of rungs to climb, be sure to wave to them as you pass them on your way up to the top.

[IF I ONLY KNEW THEN WHAT I KNOW NOW™]

LESSON 124

IN ALL HONESTY

If you tell the truth, you don't have to remember anything.
—Mark Twain

If someone knew a secret about you that could affect your life and your future choices, wouldn't you want to know about it?

Chances are you would.

So why is it, that when we know something that another should know, we find it so difficult to tell them; and often when we do, we tend to downplay it and not give them the full truth?

One of the big reasons is that we've found it's easy to tell people what they want to hear, because we don't want to hurt them or seem like the bad person.

Yet, in reality, we can end up hurting them and ourselves in the longrun.

THE LESSON TO BE LEARNED IS…

Always tell the truth.

Always.

You've got more than enough tact, diplomacy and compassion to do so in such a way that the other will know that you're doing it from a position of caring and wanting the best for them.

The old saying that for every lie you tell, you must tell five lies to cover it up, holds more truth than fiction.

:: The Lessons of Life and What They're Trying to Teach You ::

Truth is power, and to be a person who is truthful is to be someone with an enviable character.

While telling the truth may not always be easy, it is always the right thing to say.

[IF I ONLY KNEW THEN WHAT I KNOW NOW™]

LESSON 125

ONE OF LIFE'S GREATEST LESSONS

Now, if you want to get rich, you have only to produce a product or service that will give people greater use value than the price you charge for it. How rich you get will be determined by the number of people to whom you can sell this product or service.

—Earl Nightingale

You can travel to any country on the planet and you will find people who have devoted their lives to searching for ways to become successful.

Sure, one of the best paths to success is to find a need and fill it. Or create a need for people and fill it.

But, that's only part of the answer.

The real secret to success is contained in a set of principles that are so simple that most people don't even think about them.

THE LESSON TO BE LEARNED IS…

Success in this world is so easy if you have the desire and ability to work hard, you are ambitious, you consistently set attainable goals, you are a person of your word, you are dependable, you have discipline, you take massive amounts of focused and clearly defined action, and you persevere until you accomplish your goals and dreams.

See, I told you it was simple.

| LIFE'S WORDS OF WISDOM |

Act as if it were impossible to fail.

—Dorothea Brande

[IF I ONLY KNEW THEN WHAT I KNOW NOW™]

LESSON 126

WHAT YOU BELIEVE IS WHAT YOU GET

*If you don't live the life you believe,
you'll start believing the life you're living.*
—Anonymous

Sayings.

My, oh my. Everywhere you go there's a book, magazine or someone extolling the virtues of wisdom.

So why is it so hard for people to understand and apply the positive power of belief in their lives?

Fact is, these same people apply the power of belief every day, but it's been the power of lack, limitation and uncertainty in their abilities, talents and themselves to have a new and better life.

It's time to grasp the truth that *the height of one's achievement is determined by the depth of one's belief.*

THE LESSON TO BE LEARNED IS...

Are you among those who aren't living the kind of life you truly want, because you have accepted the belief that you must first see everything laid out in front of you, before you will take action and move toward your goals and dreams?

Sorry to break the news to you, friend, but life doesn't work that way.

It works by faith, belief and action.

All you have to know is what you want to do and

where you want to be. Forget the notion that you have to have everything in order before you act, because it never will be.

Right now, people are enjoying a new life, a great life, because they had a dream and went for that dream, even though they had no idea how in the world they would accomplish it.

You see, in this world right now are people who are experts in every conceivable field.

People whose only job it is to do their thing and do it well.

The majority of folks go wrong and never take action because they want to learn all they can about the subject before they begin, and then they want to do it all themselves.

The greatest leaders in politics, business, entertainment, education and the arts didn't and don't know everything there is to know about their business. Yet, they surrounded themselves with the people who do, and that's the difference between them and you; people who can bridge the gap between where you are right now and where you want to be.

So forget about having all the facts before you begin.

Stop being a victim of Analysis Paralysis.

Everything you need to accomplish your goals and dreams is inside you right now.

Have a clear picture of what you want, and your subconscious mind will take you to the people, places and events you will need to make whatever you deeply desire happen.

I'll leave you with an incredible, inspiring story.

The late Andrew Carnegie was one of the richest men on the planet when he was alive. Carnegie was one of the greatest successes the world had seen.

One day, while interviewing Carnegie, a young reporter by the name of Napoleon Hill asked Carnegie how he made his incredible fortune.

To paraphrase, the wise Carnegie told Hill that even though he was in the steel business and made his fortune from it, he knew virtually nothing about the making and selling of steel.

The young Hill was taken by surprise at such a statement.

How in the world could the richest man in the world at that time make his fortune in a business he said he knew virtually nothing about?

Carnegie replied, "By surrounding myself with people who do."

Lesson learned.

It's time to surround yourself with the right people and make your fortune.

LESSON 127

OUT WITH THE OLD AND IN WITH THE NEW

People's actions are the only true measure of their beliefs.

Take a good look at your beliefs.

I mean really examine them.

Which beliefs have you held onto for so long that they aren't doing you any good?

Why do you still have them?

Who sold you on them in the first place, and why did you come to accept them?

The answers are quite revealing, aren't they?

Most people never take the time to sit down and really think about why they have the beliefs they do.

Like living robots, they simply keep doing the same old thing over and over, day in, day out. That is, until the pain, frustration, and lack of fulfillment of the life they've been living literally shakes them by the bootstraps and they finally wake up.

THE LESSON TO BE LEARNED IS...

Have you now been awakened?

Good!

Now it's time to throw away those old, torn, worn out, broken and unworkable beliefs and replace them with new and empowering beliefs that will help you have the life you really want.

Here's what I want you to do.

Every month, six months and year, take a few minutes and examine your beliefs. Ask yourself, "Why do I believe this?" "On what foundation of fact did I base this belief?"

Many, many times, we blindly accept what our family, friends and the media tell us without even a thought as to why.

Question everything.

Hold up those beliefs to the light and look for any holes or weak seams.

Get rid of any and every belief that brings you unhappiness, fear, doubt, worry, hatred, anger, jealousy or bitterness.

Replace those beliefs with only those that support you, strengthen and motivate you and give you joy, peace, contentment, fulfillment and happiness.

Only then will you be 100% empowered to achieve any goal or dream that you desire, because now, you'll have the right beliefs to do it.

:: The Lessons of Life and What They're Trying to Teach You ::

LESSON 128

THE HIDDEN GENIE

Man is the master of thought, the molder of character, and the maker and shaper of condition, environment and destiny.

—James Allen

If I were to tell you that I knew a place where you could get a genie that would not only give you three wishes, but would give you whatever you truly desire, as much as you want, and do it for the rest off your life, would you be at all interested?

Great, because I know where you can find such a genie, and it's in a place where you've probably never even looked.

THE LESSON TO BE LEARNED IS…

Okay, so do you want to know where this genie is?

Between your ears.

That's right, your mind… your subconscious mind.

Stop for a moment a think about how many people go through their entire life carrying their genie around and never even know it or use it to bring them the incredible life that could be theirs.

Your subconscious mind never sleeps. It works nonstop 24 hours a day, 7 days a week, and its only purpose in life is to help you accomplish anything in life you truly believe and desire.

What you need to know is that there are basically two aspects to your mind: the conscious and the subconscious.

The conscious part is what you think about throughout the day. It's what you tell yourself about you (in the form of self-talk that's constantly going on throughout the day), your observations and opinions about the things you're doing, the experiences you have and the people you see, meet and interact with.

Your conscious mind is what you use to set your goals and dreams. Yet once your conscious mind has determined your goals and dreams, the powerhouse—the subconscious—takes over.

The subconscious is the most faithful and able servant you could ever wish for. For contained deep within its recesses are the powers to make your goals and dreams come true in ways no one knows.

Think of your subconscious as that faithful servant whose only job is to listen to your conscious commands—the things you constantly tell yourself—and do whatever it takes to make those conscious commands come true.

The subconscious servant doesn't care if the things you are telling it are true or not, as its job is not to ask you if they are. Its only job is to bring those people, events and circumstances to you that are in perfect harmony with the thoughts you think.

If your conscious thoughts are mostly thoughts of negativity, lack, limitation, struggle, hardship, unhappiness and limits on what you can be, do, have or experience, your subconscious servant will make sure your life is filled with those things.

In a world governed by cause and effect, how could you ask for anything different? After all, your conscious thoughts have been primarily about these things.

Yet, give your subconscious servant the command—by your dominant thoughts—that you are a great success, enjoying unlimited opportunity, wealth and constant success, and watch what happens.

Your subconscious servant will bring all those things, and many others, to you in perfect divine fashion and with absolute perfect timing.

A few things to remember if you are to get the most from your subconscious servant:

> **1.** Keep your conscious thoughts only on those things that are pure, positive and empowering; focus on that which you want, not on that which you don't want.
>
> **2.** Use positive self-talk (after all, you talk to yourself every minute of every day) and affirm that you already have the things you want to have and experience. The reason is that your subconscious servant doesn't know the difference between a real or an imagined experience. If you keep telling yourself that you're enjoying living a life of great success, wealth, fulfillment, happiness and opportunity, yet in reality right now you may not be, your subconscious servant's job is to take you from where you are to where you now say and believe you are.
>
> **3.** Think on these things as much as you can throughout the day. Two of the very best times to talk to your subconscious servant are at night just

before going to bed and first thing in the morning as soon as you awaken.

4. The more emotion and desire you place behind your conscious words and beliefs, the faster your subconscious servant will go to work for you and bring you whatever it is you truly and deeply desire. For it is the white-hot emotion of positive desire that brings whatever you desire to your life in a hurry.

I'll leave you with a poem called "My Wage," about what your genie—your subconscious servant—will do for you if only you'll follow what I've just told you and back that with desire and belief.

I bargained with Life for a penny,
And Life would pay no more,
However I begged at evening,
When I counted my scanty store.

For Life is a just employer.
It gives you whatever you ask,
But once you have set the wages,
Then it is you who must bear the task.

For I worked for a menial's wage,
Only to learn and be dismayed,
That any wage I would have asked of Life,
Life would have willingly paid.

—Jessie B. Rittenhouse

LIFE'S WORDS OF WISDOM

We learn wisdom from failure much more than from success. We often discover what will do by finding out what will not do; and probably he who never made a mistake never made a discovery.

—Samuel Smiles

LESSON 129

YOU HAVE NEVER FAILED

Men are born to succeed, not to fail.
—Henry David Thoreau

All that you ever have experienced in your life is success.

Does that sound hard to believe?

It's true.

Whatever you've done, achieved or received is the result of a deep-seated belief that it was exactly what you deserved or believed you should have.

As you just learned, your subconscious mind—your subconscious servant—only responds to the commands you give it, and those commands are given by your dominant thoughts and beliefs.

Any idea that you consciously dwell upon and think about is accepted as a command by your subconscious mind.

And you know that your subconscious servant doesn't care if the thought or belief is right or wrong, true or false, good or bad, as its only job is to make that belief come true by making that experience happen in your life.

If you dwell on sickness, problems, life's difficulties, limitation and a lack of money or opportunities, then that is exactly what you will experience.

And because that's what you been telling your subconscious servant that this is what you think success is, then

:: The Lessons of Life and What They're Trying to Teach You ::

that's exactly the kind of success it will bring you, day in and day out, as long as you keep thinking the same way.

THE LESSON TO BE LEARNED IS...

Remember, the universe operates by unchanging, immutable law.

What you sow, so also shall you reap.

Now, if you'll only change your thoughts and beliefs to prosperity, wealth, success, unlimited opportunities, happiness, joy, peace, contentment, fulfillment, understanding, wisdom, riches, opulence and fortune, then you will and you must have those things in your life.

Your subconscious mind—that genie of yours—will bring those things to you through whatever means necessary.

Some of those means may be having new thoughts and attitudes; being at the right place at the right time; connecting with the right people who can help you achieve your goals and dreams; and having the right ideas, hunches and inspirations so that when you immediately act upon them, you will have great results and success.

Just understand this: All you have to do is know exactly what you want and see it clearly and in sharp, vivid detail.

Believe that you are now enjoying that which you want, keep those thoughts in your mind constantly and let the powerhouse inside you—your subconscious mind—take over and bring whatever it is you truly want and believe, to you.

Forget about how or when it will come to you.

Just know that it will.

[IF I ONLY KNEW THEN WHAT I KNOW NOW™]

LESSON 130

THE MIRACLE THAT'S CALLED "YOU"

No man is in true health who can not stand in the free air of heaven, with his feet on God's free turf, and thank his Creator for the simple luxury of physical existence.
— T.W. Higginson

You are incredible.

You know why?

Nowhere in history, either before or after you leave this earth, will there be anyone like you.

Do you really understand that?

No one has or will ever have your talents, abilities, looks, mannerisms, personality, voice, beliefs, goals and ability to make your dreams come true like you.

No one!

Are you starting to catch my drift?

To show you the incredible odds—the most difficult you'll ever face—you've already overcome many, many years ago, I want you to comprehend this.

Of the tens of millions of possibilities of sperm that could have united with an egg to become a human, only one of those sperm did, and the person it created was you.

You know what that means?

You have faced the toughest obstacle that you will ever have to face in your life, and that was surviving the incredible odds of being born.

:: The Lessons of Life and What They're Trying to Teach You ::

Yes, the gift of life.

You made it.

Everything you do from this moment on will be easy, because you have faced life's toughest challenge and won.

THE LESSON TO BE LEARNED IS...

You see, my friend, you were created for a special reason.

You were given the most incredible talents, dreams and one-of-a-kind abilities to help you achieve the life you dream of, the life and experiences you want.

And whenever those times happen that you're not feeling so special, just remember a few things.

The first thing is to get back in touch with the power that created you. Thank it for guiding you perfectly in every part of your life.

The next thing is to forget more of yourself and think more of how you and your desires and abilities can help others.

People are all that matter.

Think about it.

You do the things you do for love, adulation, recognition or financial gain. And where do you think all those things come from?

People.

And the more you serve people, the greater will be your rewards.

A very rich man once said, "Your rewards in life are in direct proportion to the amount of service you give to others."

You want more wealth and happiness?

Give more service to others.

You want more fame and recognition?

Give more of yourself to the world.

Use your life to change people's lives, and they will shower you with more fame, fortune, wealth, opportunity and happiness than you ever dreamed possible.

That's what can happen when you give to the world, the miracle called "You."

:: The Lessons of Life and What They're Trying to Teach You ::

LESSON 131

LET'S OPEN YOUR OWNER'S MANUAL

*All I have seen teaches me to trust the Creator
for all I have not seen.*
—Ralph Waldo Emerson

There has never, nor will there ever be, anyone just like you. Your voice, looks and personality are all uniquely yours.

And if you're such an incredible creation with gifts, talents and abilities that no one else has or will ever have, why on earth would you want to compare, compete and be like someone else? This world is yours to enjoy, give your abilities to and reap the bountiful rewards that are yours to keep.

You see, your Creator knows exactly what it takes to make you happy and fulfilled. After all, It created you. And if It created you, It wrote the owners manual for your operation.

THE LESSON TO BE LEARNED IS...

When you trust the Creator for the direction of your life, It opens your owner's manual and uses it to guide you in the direction It knows you need to go. By following Its direction, you are always at the perfect place, at the perfect time and with the perfect opportunities with the perfect people.

Most people have such incredible talents and abilities that if they used them, they would have the kind of life they dream of. Instead, they ignore, neglect and simply forget about their gifts and talents and settle for their second or third choice.

These people erroneously believe that doing what they are talented at is too easy, so in their minds they somehow adopt the belief that it can't possibly be the right thing for them to do.

They believe that life must be hard. That anything good must come from toil and difficulty and, many times, unenjoyable work.

However, when it comes to being rewarded as a result of using your talents, nothing could be further from the truth.

When you ignore your gifts and abilities, your Creator gets your attention by putting this dull ache and feeling of unfulfillment in your life.

Try to ignore it with all your might, but this dull ache and feeling of unfulfillment will not go away until you start using your talents and abilities in the way the Creator meant for you to use them.

That's why it's been said that most people are afraid of dying because they really never lived.

And the sad fact is that most people go to their graves with their music still inside them.

Why not let your music play to this world?

Why not use every gift, talent and ability you have to the very fullest of your God-given ability?

It's time once and for all to make your life a beautiful symphony to listen to and enjoy.

LESSON 132

EVERYTHING IN LIFE HAPPENS FOR A REASON

A careful inventory of all your past experiences may disclose the startling fact that everything has happened for the best.
—Napoleon Hill

So many people think that things happen by accident or chance!

Yet these are the same people who believe they have little, if any, power to direct their destiny.

Every decision you have ever made has brought you to a place right now in your life of helping mold you into the person that you have become.

Just try taking one little experience out of everything that has happened to you—at the time, happy or painful—and you will see that you would not have become who you are unless you had that experience.

THE LESSON TO BE LEARNED IS…

Once you see that every decision you've made and every result you've felt has made you what you are, you see that nothing happens by accident.

There's always a reason behind it, and those reasons are to help teach you and make you grow into what you are.

That's only the first step.

The second step is that now that you know that, you consciously give more thought to the life you want to live and direct your goals, dreams, energy and actions only in the direction of that life and nowhere else.

By doing so, you guarantee yourself that you will experience only those learning experiences and growing lessons that stem from your having chosen the life you want and not something else.

You are here for a reason, and whatever happens to you happens for a reason.

Embrace it.

LESSON 133

YOU WILL CATCH MORE FLIES WITH HONEY THAN WITH VINEGAR

*Develop the attitude of gratitude
and your life will never be the same.*

How does it make you feel when someone goes out of their way and says "thank you" for something you did or said to them?

If your self-image and self-esteem is strong and healthy, it makes you feel great. If it isn't, it makes you feel uncomfortable, and you show that discomfort by downplaying and minimizing those things that caused others to be thankful to you.

But wherever you travel to and whomever you meet, you'll find that one of the strongest needs of any human is the need to feel needed, wanted and appreciated.

And if you can help make them feel that way, you'll have more friends, joyous experiences and happiness than you can shake a stick at.

People want you to praise them and love them for who they are and what they do.

We all have that need, and there's absolutely nothing wrong with it. And we develop the ability and desire to praise others when we embrace the attitude of gratitude in ourselves and in our lives.

THE LESSON TO BE LEARNED IS…

Be thankful for everything that has, is and ever will happen in your life. For every one of those things has made you who and what you are.

Kind words of gratitude are like honey that is sweet to hear and even sweeter to taste.

For you will win more people to get behind you and your dreams if you will only show them kindness and gratitude for everything they do for you.

One of the most powerful lessons my mother instilled in me was to always say thank you for anything anybody does for me.

I can't even begin to tell you how many doors to success in life have been opened to me as a result of the kindness that I showed to other people.

The same can and will happen for you too.

Send thank-you letters, cards or even emails to people who do anything for you. You'll be amazed at their response, because so few people take the time to think of others.

Say thanks to someone if they open a door for you, say a kind word or give a compliment. Take just one day and see how many things you can be thankful to someone for. You will be surprised at how many you will find.

Praise and gratitude are natural expressions of being human.

It comes so easy; yet, because of fear of what others might think of us, most people keep all the praise for others inside; a place where it does no one any good.

Let your praise and gratitude out and get ready for the unexpected.

LIFE'S WORDS OF WISDOM

First of all, it is important to understand that failure feelings—fear, anxiety, lack of self-confidence—do not spring from some heavenly oracle.... They originate from your own mind. They are indicative only of attitudes of mind within you—not of external facts which are rigged against you. They mean only that you are underestimating your own abilities, overestimating and exaggerating the nature of the difficulty before you, and that you are reactivating memories of past failures rather than of past successes. That is all they mean and all that they signify. They do not pertain to or represent the truth concerning future events, but only your own mental attitude about the future event.

—Dr. Maxwell Maltz

LESSON 134

GO WHERE OTHERS FEAR, AND LIFE WILL MEET YOU THERE WITH REWARDS OTHERS CAN ONLY DREAM ABOUT

If you'll do the things that others won't, you'll have things that others can't.

One lesson Life teaches is if you hoard your gifts, talents and abilities, few if any successes will come your way.

You and Life are perfectly matched partners. Life is always ready to give you what you want. However, you must be willing to give Life what it wants.

Nature's orders are that it must answer your dreams and desires so long as those dreams and desires are backed by a specific plan, belief, faith in yourself and action taken for the achievement of those dreams and desires.

If you choose not to dream, choose not to believe, choose not to have faith and choose not to act, you must pay the price.

Heartache, disappointment, emptiness, anger, frustration, worry, doubt and fear are only some of the consequences of those choices.

Ah, but dare to dream, dare to believe, dare to have faith and dare to act, and Life will reward you beyond any measure of your comprehension.

Basil King has said, "Be bold and mighty forces will come to your aid." Fortune and greatness do indeed favor and embrace the bold.

THE LESSON TO BE LEARNED IS…

Yes, life is filled with people, just like you, who were afraid to step out on the limb and try something new, but did so anyway. They had just enough belief in themselves to take action towards the destination of their dreams.

Yet, all it took was just that little bit of action, and they left the unhappy others behind. These extraordinary people, just like you, took action because deep in their heart they realized that you can only pick the fruit if you go out on the limb.

As the Bible says, "The harvest is plenty but the workers are few."

It's time to gather your bountiful harvest.

LESSON 135

KNOW WHEN TO LET GO

People can grab and hold onto the things that will make them happy, if only they'll let go of the things that keep making them unhappy.

One of the hardest things for people to do is to let go.

Whether it's an unworkable relationship, friendship, dead-end job or memories of the past of what might have been or could have been if only you had done this or that, letting go is just downright difficult.

But why?

Well, the thought of losing something—even if it's losing something painful—can cause us more discomfort than the actual thing we need to let go of. It's twice as tough for many people if they don't have something or someone else to takes its place.

It's the uncertainty of not knowing what will replace what they need to lose that keeps them stuck in quicksand of stagnation, emptiness and deep unhappiness.

THE LESSON TO BE LEARNED IS...

Everyone and everything in your life has a season for you to enjoy them.

Some of those seasons can be for the rest of your life. For others, those seasons are brief.

Yet just as the seasons will change and bring us a new start and a new year, so too will letting go of the past allow the freshness of things new and exciting enter your life.

But you must let go of those things that are causing you pain and unhappiness before new things and experiences will come into your life and take their place.

In life, timing is everything. So, too, is knowing when to let go.

[IF I ONLY KNEW THEN WHAT I KNOW NOW™]

LESSON 136

BECOME THE EXCEPTIONAL PERSON

*He who undervalues himself is justly
undervalued by others.*

—William Hazlitt

People all over the world admire exceptional people, the rare individuals who do great things with their life and for other people.

Watching from the sidelines, we find it easy to think that these people are gifted in some special way that allows them to easily have the kind of life so many people admire.

But that's not true.

Every single human has gifts, talents and abilities that are uniquely their own and not shared by anyone else.

And you are one of those exceptional people.

The only difference between you and them is that right now, they've just had a bit more belief in themselves that's allowed them that little extra to do the uncommon and become the exceptional.

THE LESSON TO BE LEARNED IS…

To live an exceptional life and achieve exceptional things, you must first live by a creed that the exceptional embrace.

That is…

- To live the exceptional life, you must accept only the exceptional.

- To live the exceptional life, you must experience only the exceptional.

- To live the exceptional life, you must expect the exceptional to happen to you.

- To live the exceptional life, you must associate and spend time with the exceptional, for their positive influence will rub off on you in many wonderful ways.

Imagine yourself as being exceptional.

Feel what it would feel like to be the exceptional.

Allow powerful and positive exceptional thoughts to fill your mind.

Hear the accolades and praise from others, for you are the exceptional person they admire and look up to.

I've got great news for you.

You truly are that person.

There are no exceptions!

LIFE'S WORDS OF WISDOM

Take time to laugh, it is the music of the soul
Take time to think, it is the source of power
Take time to play, it is the source of perpetual youth.
Take time to read, it is the fountain of wisdom
Take time to pray, it is the greatest power on earth.
Take time to love and be loved, it is a God-given privilege.
Take time to be friendly, it is the road to happiness.
Take time to give, life is too short to be selfish.
Take time to work, it is the price of success.

—Anonymous

[IF I ONLY KNEW THEN WHAT I KNOW NOW™]

LESSON 137

SEE THE BIG PICTURE

*As little letters most tire the eyes,
so do little affairs most disturb us.*
—Michel de Montaigne

Over the course of time, people have found the most innovative ways to frustrate themselves. One of the most effective is by focusing their time, energy and attention on the small details in life.

Seems that fine print was created by those chronically frustrated who want others to share in their same misery.

To be sure, details do make the difference, for not paying attention to the fine print can cause more than a few headaches down the road.

However, where many people get sidetracked is by using the fine print and details as a way to keep themselves stuck on the same roller coaster, without ever being able to get off and enjoy the other rides of life.

THE LESSON TO BE LEARNED IS...

It's high time for you to understand the big picture of how everything works in harmony and perfect order.

You don't need to know all the details about something before you use it. Just begin and have fun learning as you go.

See the big picture in everything you do. Start expanding your thinking—and not just to your job, your hometown and what you hear from friends, see on television and in the movies or read in books, newspapers, magazines or on the Internet.

There's a whole new world just waiting for you to explore it, and you begin by opening the steel door to your mind that has been shut too tightly for much too long.

Allow some fresh air and sunlight in, and watch how fast you grow!

Details tend to attract the perfectionist personality, and especially those who are afraid to take chances in all areas of their life.

After all, details are safe; and the fewer chances someone takes, the safer they feel. And the more details they create, the busier they can be and the more insulated they become.

It's time for you to know the details yet not get stuck in them.

It's time for you to become a global wonder.

I'm talking two wonders here.

The global wonder you become by using your life to change your world and ultimately, that world around you; and, of course, the global wonder you become by your hunger to have, be, do and experience more of the great life that awaits you.

LIFE'S WORDS OF WISDOM

The search for happiness is one of the chief sources of unhappiness.

—Eric Hoffer

LESSON 138

THE BIG CHASE

*Happiness is as a butterfly, which, when pursued,
is always beyond our grasp, but which,
if you will sit down quietly, may alight upon you.*
—Nathaniel Hawthorne

Why is that many times in life, what you spend a lot of time chasing seems to elude you? Then, once you quit chasing it, like a shadow it chases you?

This is so true, especially when it comes to relationships and money.

For how many times has it been that when you didn't have a relationship and constantly gave your thoughts to finding that right person, you met with frustration after frustration?

Yet, after you quit being so desperate to be in a relationship, the right relationship—with the right person—found you.

Then there's money and chasing after the almighty dollar (or whatever denomination of currency you're after).

At one time or another—maybe still—you wanted more of it. Perhaps a lot more of it.

So you spent countless, days, months, and even years, racking your brain trying to think of easy ways to make a fortune. For one of the hardest things about making a lot of money seems to be looking for the easy ways to do it.

Finally you got frustrated and started focusing your time and energies on the things you do best. Using your natural talents to your fullest potential and in ways that help the greatest numbers of people.

And what happened?

The rewards, wealth and success started flowing to you.

You stopped chasing it and it started chasing you.

THE LESSON TO BE LEARNED IS...

Whatever it is you want, wants you; but you must give up the need to run after it and let it come to you in its own timing.

Remember how your subconscious mind works to bring you perfect matches to your most dominant thoughts and beliefs?

So if your thoughts are constantly about getting something you don't have, you are giving a powerful command to your mind that you don't have the thing you want and its job is to keep you wanting that which you don't have because your thoughts are constantly focused on that. Thinking that way sends out the message: "What you don't have, you won't have."

Whereas, keep your mind on believing that you *already* have the thing you want, you are enjoying it and are thankful for it, then go off and do the things you do best that serve the greatest numbers of people and your subconscious mind will bring you to the people, places and events that will help you have that which you've deeply desired.

It's okay. Go ahead and take a quick look behind you.

Your shadow of success is following you wherever you go.

LIFE'S WORDS OF WISDOM

The greatest mistake you can make in life is to be continually fearing you will make one.

—Elbert Hubbard

[IF I ONLY KNEW THEN WHAT I KNOW NOW™]

LESSON 139

THIS JUST IN: IT'S OKAY TO GET EXCITED!

Let us be of good cheer, remembering that the misfortunes hardest to bear are those which never come.

—James Russell Lowell

People are something.

When asked if they're excited about what might happen or the outcome or possibilities of a future event they want to happen, so many times they dread giving you a response. As if, getting one's hopes up will change the outcome of the event.

Yes, these are the folks who love to say, with measured skepticism, "Oh, we'll see" or "I just don't want to get too excited or get my hopes up too high—that way, I won't be disappointed."

What's that all about?

It's as if they're anticipating defeat even before they get started.

How in the heck do they ever expect to win with that kind of negative and defeatist attitude?

These usually are the people who who've set their sights too low or have too low an opinion of their self-worth to make happen whatever they want in life.

Those who answer, "I don't know, we'll see," are those who should be saying, "If I only believe enough, it will happen."

THE LESSON TO BE LEARNED IS...

Those who won't—and notice I didn't say can't, because every one can—allow themselves to get excited for fear of letdown or disappointment usually have only one set of reference points to indicate success: Reaching that goal in that particular way and at that particular time.

If you hear me talking to you, it's high time for you to stop setting yourself up for feeling lousy, unexcited and dispassionate about life and the direction it's going.

The trick is for you to set up—in advance—a series of success markers so that even if you didn't reach the original goal you wanted in the particular way you wanted, you would still consider yourself and the venture a success from the lessons learned.

By doing so, the lessons you will have learned can propel you closer than ever to the goal you seek or maybe even a goal you should've been seeking all along.

And even whenever a series of events—which seem like failures and disappointments—come your way, embrace them, because in reality, those apparent failures will become your teachers and blessings.

Many times, when something doesn't work out as planned, your true goal and desire reveals itself.

It's that "aha" moment that can change your life for the best.

:: The Lessons of Life and What They're Trying to Teach You ::

LESSON 140

LEARN FROM OTHERS' MISTAKES, BECAUSE YOU'LL NEVER LIVE LONG ENOUGH TO MAKE THEM YOURSELF

I have learned more from my mistakes than from my successes.

—Sir Humphry Davy

That advice has been around for a couple of centuries. Still, people don't care to listen to it.

In a way, it makes for great entertainment because it gives television and the other media an endless supply of material.

You know how we are, we'll see people on these shows or read about them and all their problems and mistakes they make and in our easy chairs we sit back and think, "When will these people ever learn?"

Then after the show is over, we start worrying about all the junk in our lives because of the unwise decisions we've made and will continue to make but don't need to, when we simply could've learned from the mistakes of others.

THE LESSON TO BE LEARNED IS...

As far as I can tell, there has never been a perfect person created, and it looks like the next model of human won't be perfect either, so relax. We all make mistakes.

However, while mistakes can be powerful teachers, the type and frequency of the mistake has a lot to say about the person making it. For if you don't learn from your mistakes, you're bound to constantly repeat them.

Like the fairest of all teachers, Life keeps presenting the lessons you are ignoring—in the form of the mistakes you are making—many times in different forms. And those mistakes will keep returning and repeating until you learn what you're supposed to learn so you can move on to the next level of your growth.

Or could I be mistaken?

| LIFE'S WORDS OF WISDOM |

Man is the richest whose pleasures are the cheapest.

—Henry David Thoreau

[IF I ONLY KNEW THEN WHAT I KNOW NOW™]

LESSON 141

CHOOSE CAREFULLY THOSE FROM WHOM YOU SEEK ADVICE

If you want to learn how to make money, speak to someone who has a lot of it.

If you needed a haircut, would you go to your auto mechanic?

Okay, if you needed an operation, would you go to your accountant?

Then why is it that when you want advice on how to make money, you keep talking to people who don't have a lot of it?

Doesn't make sense now, does it?

Yet we still listen to the well-intentioned, yet often misguided advice from family, friends, co-workers and even those "experts" who write for all those money-oriented publications. You'd be surprised to learn that many of those experts dispensing advice to the masses are themselves still looking for someone to show them how it's done.

THE LESSON TO BE LEARNED IS...

If you tell your friends and family that you want to make a million dollars, chances are they'd look at you like you've really gone off the deep end.

However, tell that to someone who has a lot of money and they'll tell you how they did it.

The person with a lot of money understands where you are coming from, because unless they inherited their fortune, they started where you are too.

They know the pitfalls, struggles and obstacles you will face.

They also know how to avoid mistakes, because they probably made a lot of them on their way to the top.

Wealthy people, like most any experts, are surprisingly easy to approach and talk to.

There seems to be this philanthropic desire in people who have achieved great success to want to give back to others—and not just handing out cash—the blessings they've been given.

They do this by helping others—people just like you—achieve success so you'll be able to do it for someone else down the road.

Always seek out the real experts.

Those who have achieved the things you want to achieve.

The time you save will be worth a fortune.

[IF I ONLY KNEW THEN WHAT I KNOW NOW™]

LESSON 142

YESTERDAY'S SUCCESS IS LIKE YESTERDAY'S NEWS—QUICKLY FORGOTTEN

If you have been wise and successful I congratulate you; unless you are unable to forget how successful you have been, then I pity you.
—Napoleon Hill

What a great feeling it is to have worked long and hard for a goal and then to have achieved it.

You want the feeling to last forever, but somehow it doesn't. It's as if your mind is telling you "Okay, Pal, we've achieved this goal, so what's next?"

Where people become "a has been" is when they remain in the past, bask in their past accomplishments (or their "one-hit wonder") and stop there. The desire is gone to grow, become more, do greater work, learn and expand.

THE LESSON TO BE LEARNED IS...

In life, you can be the greatest success but that doesn't mean much because all others care about is *today* and for you to prove yourself *now*.

It's as if those other successes in your life never happened.

The great news is, that's fine, because as a creative person you are constantly growing and getting better and better each day.

:: The Lessons of Life and What They're Trying to Teach You ::

Your awareness is constantly expanding and, as a result, so are you talents and abilities, thereby increasing your value and making who you are and what you do more in demand to other people.

When it comes to having worked hard—or perhaps I'll say, not having worked at all, because once you love what you're doing, you'll never work another day in your life—take time to enjoy all the success of having achieved that goal.

But don't get caught up in the celebration too long.

You have many more goals and dreams you want to achieve, and Life's success train waits for no one.

Get on it and enjoy the ride.

You don't have time to read yesterday's newspaper.

You're busy creating today's headlines.

[IF I ONLY KNEW THEN WHAT I KNOW NOW™]

LESSON 143

GETTING OUT OF THE HOLDING PATTERN

Fortune favors the bold but abandons the timid.
—Latin proverb

Ever notice whenever an airport's busy and planes are backed up waiting to take off and land, how the planes in the sky will keep circling the airport, burning off fuel, until the control tower gives them clearance to land?

Your life is much the same way.

Think of your thoughts and beliefs as the plane marked "What Is" and the runway below marked "What Can Be."

By keeping your mind on the thoughts you've been thinking and the beliefs you've been believing, you will keep circling in the air waiting for clearance to land on the runway of the great new life and experiences that await you.

But unless you get out of the holding pattern, your plane will never be able to land.

It's time we change that.

THE LESSON TO BE LEARNED IS...

Let's talk about the things you find yourself constantly thinking about. Do those things feel so normal by now that you've become used to them?

Or are they the thoughts and beliefs of the things you truly want? Are they bringing you happiness and joy? Are they things you're committed to?

:: The Lessons of Life and What They're Trying to Teach You ::

Most people will never ask themselves those questions. And if they do, they are surprised at how many years of their lives have gone by, circling the runway waiting to land.

So many people live their lives in a foggy haze, and this foggy haze of consciousness prevents them from imagining what can be instead of what they keep watching daily in their lives.

You can't blame them.

Keeping one's mind on the daily and knowable starts to feel really comfortable quickly—even if it brings unhappiness.

Your life doesn't have to be that way.

Starting tomorrow, begin your day by waking up with new thoughts that will empower you.

New and different thoughts that focus on the "what could be."

It's those "what could be's" that will ignite something inside of you that's going to make you feel different.

And those different feelings will inspire you to take action.

So get your plane ready to land.

The holding pattern ends when the belief and action begin.

[IF I ONLY KNEW THEN WHAT I KNOW NOW™]

LESSON 144

THINKING ABOUT YOUR PROBLEM WON'T CHANGE IT, BUT ACTION WILL

Weak is he who permits his thoughts to control his actions: Strong is he who forces his actions to control his thoughts.
—Og Mandino

How many times have you thought and thought about changing some aspect of your life, yet, something always seems to keep you stuck where you are?

When you think about the change, it makes sense on all fronts, but actually doing it is really the toughest part.

THE LESSON TO BE LEARNED IS…

To solve a problem or change any part of your life requires you to do but one thing: Take action.

Taking action changes your emotion about the very thing you wanted to change for so long but felt you couldn't.

Action has a wonderful way of neutralizing fear, and it gives you new and powerfully positive emotions to go along with the action you've just taken.

Remember the words "Do it now," whenever you're thinking about changing some aspect of your life but feel stuck.

But don't just remember those words.

Whenever you tell yourself "Do it now," take action and watch what happens.

:: The Lessons of Life and What They're Trying to Teach You ::

The mountain you've created in your thoughts that's been stopping you will disappear like it was never even there in the first place.

[IF I ONLY KNEW THEN WHAT I KNOW NOW™]

LESSON 145

TIME TO BE THE RIDER AND NOT THE HORSE

If you don't have goals, you're bound for the rest of your life to work for someone who does.

—Anonymous

Millions of people have found out that working for someone else can be a great thing.

You get to go to a job, you probably get some sort of benefits, you get to meet new people, you have a schedule that has been pre-set for you, you get a few weeks of vacation off each year and you get a regular paycheck for the work you do.

And you get to make someone else's dreams come true.

For most people, that's okay and the trade off is something they can live with.

However, for others, the price is too high to pay for neglecting their own dreams just for the security of having a regular job.

How about you?

THE LESSON TO BE LEARNED IS…

Unless you work for the handful of companies who really treat their employees well or have the realistic opportunity to achieve your highest goals within the confines of that company, the only way you will have the life you want is to be your own boss.

Own your own business.

Anything else simply means you're the horse and somebody else is riding you to the finish line in the race to make the other person's dreams and goals come true.

That's too high a price to pay for not using your incredible talents and abilities, because your employers don't recognize them—or if they do, there's simply no room for you to develop them the way you want to develop them.

Sure, being your own boss and having your own business can seem a bit daunting at first. After all, it's something new, and you may not have a whole lot of references from which to base your beliefs and decisions.

But like all other business owners, you quickly learn and become excellent at what you do.

Great success is sure to follow.

To live a life of no limits and on your own terms, you must be willing to go in the opposite direction of the crowd.

Yes, in the opposite direction of the sheep.

For, you can be the best employee your employer has ever seen, but you will always be limited in the amount of money you will make or the opportunities you will have by the limits and politics of that company.

All variables you can't control.

Take charge of your life and your destiny by following your heart and deepest desires, and you can do it by having the business called "You, Inc."

LIFE'S WORDS OF WISDOM

Every time one man puts an idea across, he finds ten men who thought of it before he did—but they only thought of it.

—Anonymous

[IF I ONLY KNEW THEN WHAT I KNOW NOW™]

LESSON 146

THE WORLD IS FULL OF TALKERS

The world is moving so fast these days that the man who says it can't be done is generally interrupted by someone doing it.

—Harry Emerson Fosdick

We live in a world filled with talkers.

People who talk a great game, but rarely follow through on what they say. You listen to them, believe them and trust in them. And so often the same thing happens: "Why didn't you do what you said you'd do?"

But, not all people are like that.

You'll find there are those who are people of their word, and if they tell you something, you can take their word to the bank, because they'll live up to it.

THE LESSON TO BE LEARNED IS...

Count yourself among the smartest if you adopt the attitude that the only thing you hear is what others do, not what they *say* they'll do.

This is a world is full of talkers who'll tell you what you want to hear, when you want to hear it.

Words may be sweet, but actions are sweeter.

If you can't do something, don't tell someone you will.

They'll respect you more for being honest and up front.

Remember, all you have is your word, and the only way to honor the power of your word is through actions.

[IF I ONLY KNEW THEN WHAT I KNOW NOW™]

LESSON 147

THE THING YOU PREPARE FOR IS OFTEN THE THING THAT NEVER COMES

I am an old man and have known a great many troubles, but most of them never happened.
—Mark Twain

I wish I could calculate how much time and precious energy people have spent preparing for something that never happens.

So many times, we get ourselves excited and worked up preparing for or anticipating a situation or event that never comes, or if it does, it turns out to be very different from what we expected.

THE LESSON TO BE LEARNED IS...

Take a good look at this thing called worry.

It has been estimated, that of the things you worry about, over 95% never happen.

Almost all your worries are imaginary and will never happen!

Of the 5% worries that do happen, 3% are nowhere near what we imagine they would be, and the other 2% are things we can't control.

So what in the heck is all the fuss about worrying about anything?

The way to eliminate worry from your life is to prepare for the best.

:: The Lessons of Life and What They're Trying to Teach You ::

Visualize and feel the best and the desired outcome and focus on that. Forget the steps you believe you will need to take you to have what you want. Focus on and feel only the result. Then, when things are presented to you, remember they come only one at a time and you can easily handle them.

Anything beyond that, forget it.

It's not worth worrying about.

LIFE'S WORDS OF WISDOM

Too often what we read and profess becomes a part of our libraries and vocabularies instead of becoming a part of our lives.

—Napoleon Hill and
W. Clement Stone

[IF I ONLY KNEW THEN WHAT I KNOW NOW™]

LESSON 148

TELL EVERYONE WHAT YOU'RE GOING TO DO, BUT FIRST SHOW THEM

It's easier to say what you'll do than do what you say.

We humans are an excitable bunch.

Why, even before something actually happens, we go off and tell all kinds of folks that it will, many times only to find out that it doesn't, hasn't or won't.

Then comes all the egg on our faces of having to explain why it didn't happen.

After a while, you'd think we'd get the message.

THE LESSON TO BE LEARNED IS...

In life, you can plan, plan, plan. Take action, action, action. However, if the timing for whatever you want isn't right—meaning other people's dreams get answered at the same time yours does—then your desires and goals are most likely going to be delayed.

So as you patiently wait for all things to work together for the good of everyone involved, keep your goals and dreams quiet from people.

Only tell the very select and trusted few who you know are behind you and understand how being successful often means being delayed but never denied.

The longer you can keep quiet whatever you're going crazy to tell everyone about, the faster you will achieve it.

And I think I know why.

I call it the Power Secrecy Vacuum Principle, and it has amazing power. Here's how...

Let's say you have a dream to accomplish; a very significant and important goal.

In the past, you'd probably tell whoever would listen to you about it, and as a result, much of the excitement about achieving that goal and then being able to tell everyone about it wears off.

The result is, you lose the excitement that would've driven you to that goal quicker because of the burning desire inside you to keep it secret, accomplish it so you could show and tell people, "Hey, look at what I just accomplished!"

However, by keeping your goals secret, you now have something inside you that will always be pushing you to accomplish that goal in a hurry, because the inherent human desire for approval and recognition is so strong that it won't let you keep things quiet for very long unless you either achieve it or blurt it out.

Nature abhors a vacuum and is always seeking to fill things in your life. And when you have strong goals and deep desires, Nature wants you to achieve those things and then move on the next things to achieve.

Remember, look at how long you've been blurting things out and look at what's happened.

Try keeping things quiet and watch how fast you achieve whatever it is you truly desire.

LESSON 149

WHAT YOU OWN MAY EVENTUALLY OWN YOU

One of life's hardest jobs is keeping up with the easy payments.

—Anonymous

As people get smarter, more efficient and more civilized, they also get deeper in debt.

Those incredible time-saving devices that people ponder in amazement as to how people 50 years ago could have lived without them, all cost money. After all, you've got to have it now, don't you?

And for those who are driven to keep up with the neighbors, if you're quiet, you can almost hear them say, "It's just so hard to get ahead in life. Our neighbors keep buying things we can't afford."

So here we are.

With life getting easier and easier with all the stuff we buy, why are so many people so chronically frustrated, empty and unhappy?

Could be that what they own is now owning them.

THE LESSON TO BE LEARNED IS...

If you're not careful, what you must have, what you think you need and what you ultimately buy will eventually own you and your lifestyle.

Debt puts you in the position of constant owing. It steals your freedom and forces you to make choices and changes in your life that can be very uncomfortable.

Take a good look at the things you need and the things you want.

It's the things you want that can own you.

Your life is much too valuable to be owned and directed by something you think you have to buy.

| LIFE'S WORDS OF WISDOM |

*The less people speak of their greatness
the more we think of it.*

—Francis Bacon

LESSON 150

THINGS ARE NEVER QUITE WHAT THEY FIRST APPEAR TO BE

When there's something you desire, isn't it amazing just how perfect everything seems?

Our wants have a way of blinding us to the realities of those wants.

Jobs first appear ideal and people too good to be true. And without much thought, people go right ahead and act on their emotions and first impressions. And far too often, they suffer the consequences.

THE LESSON TO BE LEARNED IS...

The wise person is the one who'll wait patiently and observe before making any major decision.

Each time you come back and consider that which is important for you to make a decision about, you'll gain a greater level of awareness.

You'll see things after the third encounter that you never even noticed on the first. And as you let things progress at their own pace, you'll feel the decision being formulated inside you, without even much conscious thought. Once you get the answer, act on it immediately.

Good decisions are like fine wine: never rushed and always enjoyable to experience.

[IF I ONLY KNEW THEN WHAT I KNOW NOW™]

LESSON 151

YOU'RE ALWAYS BECOMING A NEW PERSON

*The ideal life is in our blood and will never be still.
Sad will be the day for any man when he becomes
contented with the thoughts he is thinking and the deeds
he is doing—where there is not forever at the doors
of his soul some great desire to do something larger,
which he knows that he was meant and made to do.*
—Phillips Brooks

Look at how much your life has changed in just one year.

Yet isn't it easy to think that your life has always been this way and that things rarely seem to change?

Yes, you may be in the same job or relationship you were in last year, but you can be certain that you are constantly changing.

THE LESSON TO BE LEARNED IS...

Many people are uncomfortable at the thought of changing anything in their life and they go to great lengths to keep things just the way they are, thank you very much.

Sorry folks, but there are some things you don't have much control over, and one of them is the desire inside you to not accept less than your best.

Until you give everything your best and allow yourself to become what you deeply desire, you'll always feel empty, regardless of what you do and what you own.

Thank your lucky stars that you have this feeling inside you.

Your Creator knows—far better than you or anyone else—what you need to do to make you happy.

Allow yourself to become the new and ever-growing person you know you can be.

A year from now, you will be smiling that you did.

LIFE'S WORDS OF WISDOM

Many people won't make commitments because of the fear those commitments will own and control them.

[IF I ONLY KNEW THEN WHAT I KNOW NOW™]

LESSON 152

TAKE WHAT YOU HAVE AND GET STARTED

If you wait for the perfect moment when all is safe and assured, it may never arrive.

Mountains will not be climbed, races won, or lasting happiness achieved.

—Maurice Chevalier

The best time and place for you to start living your dream is where you are in your life right now.

I know, it's easy to fall victim to thinking that, once you get that new job, new car, house, more money, better relationship or more experience, you'll begin to go for that dream you've always talked about.

But that day never seems to come.

Quickly, a month, year, many years and finally, your life goes by and you have nothing to show for it except a plate full of excuses.

THE LESSON TO BE LEARNED IS...

Stop kidding yourself.

The best time to have the life you want is right now, not tomorrow or next week.

Take what you have and begin right there. That's exactly what the world's most successful people did and look at where they are.

:: The Lessons of Life and What They're Trying to Teach You ::

The world is full of stories of people who started with far less than you have right now and took the little they had and turned it and their lives into something incredible.

Start thinking of how your life would be and how you would feel if you achieved whatever it is you deeply desire to achieve.

Feel and see the rewards as if it's happening right now.

Give your mind enough rewards—reasons you want to achieve the things you do—and it will propel you with the motivation and belief you'll need to achieve and experience those things.

[IF I ONLY KNEW THEN WHAT I KNOW NOW™]

LESSON 153

OPEN THE FLOODGATES

One person with belief is equal to a force of ninety-nine who have only interests.
—John Stuart Mill

Have you ever seen Boulder Dam?

Without a doubt, it's one of the most marvelous works of human power and ingenuity.

For a moment, I want you to think of your life and what you've experienced thus far as being like an engineer who controls the switch as to how much water flows from a great dam. Here's why…

THE LESSON TO BE LEARNED IS…

In the past, your belief in yourself has been the control mechanism for how much happiness, riches, rewards and great experiences have flowed from the dam into the river of experience called your life.

Now, I want you to see your life as right now standing on the top of the dam.

As you look down on one side of the dam, you see only little puddles of water—that's right, the tiny amount of riches you've experienced because of your past belief.

But when you look at the other side of the dam, you, see all the humongous water and get a sense of its immense force and power just waiting to be released into the other side. And into your life.

:: The Lessons of Life and What They're Trying to Teach You ::

The water behind that wall is all the incredible experiences that life has waiting for you right now. The way you release those new experiences to come flooding into your life is by your belief. The greater your belief, the faster the waters of opportunity will come flooding to you.

Open the floodgates with the unshakable belief in yourself that you can have the life you've always dreamed of.

Always know that the greater your belief, the more the waters of success will flood their way to you.

| LIFE'S WORDS OF WISDOM |

Every noble work is at first impossible.

—Thomas Carlyle

[IF I ONLY KNEW THEN WHAT I KNOW NOW™]

LESSON 154

ALL YOU NEED IS ONE HIT

*It takes just one event to change
the course of a life forever.*

Year after year, people go to work, work hard and come home with a paycheck that always reminds them there is always too much month left at the end of the check.

For some, life is somewhat easier.

They're able to buy many of things they want, yet, they're always left with the feeling of not really getting ahead and having the kind of life they want.

Then there are the others...

THE LESSON TO BE LEARNED IS...

The folks who have hit paydirt.

Those we read about and watch on television, who are living the life we think we want.

They're doing it because they created their hit record and bestseller.

And no, you don't have to be a musician, author or television or movie star to do it.

All you need to do is what the late Earl Nightingale said: "To be successful and outstanding at something, we don't have to come up with something new; we need only find ways of doing it better."

And here's what will happen when you do that.

You will become one of a kind, and people will seek you and your services.

Not only that, you will be offered opportunities for things you can't even now imagine.

From those opportunities, you will be able to convert them into something that will pay off fabulously.

All it takes is a hit.

The kind you have inside you, to make happen.

LESSON 155

TAKE THE TIME AND GET AWAY

The world is a great book, of which they who never stir from home read only one page.
—Saint Augustine of Hippo

Why is it that so many people complain about their boring and uneventful lives and do little, if anything, to change them?

THE LESSON TO BE LEARNED IS...

Think back to a time when you were really stressed out about something. The months, and maybe years, of the same old routine and pressures were just too much for you to bear any longer.

So you got away.

You were only gone for a few days, but did it ever do you a world of good!

Sure, you came back to the same situation you left, but this time with a clear head and a whole new attitude.

That time away made all the difference.

We are designed to work, rest and play, and to do all three on a regular basis.

But too many of us don't.

Too much of one throws the other two off balance. And by now, you know how important balance is to your happiness and success.

[IF I ONLY KNEW THEN WHAT I KNOW NOW™]

You need to get away, and you need to do it often.

But not just in your area or state.

Expand your horizons and your life and explore.

Check out any of the other states or, better still, travel overseas.

You can read and watch all you want about other countries and their people. However, you'll never know what you're missing until you experience it firsthand.

Give yourself the gift of allowing yourself to experience more than you have.

LIFE'S WORDS OF WISDOM

It is never too late to be what you might have been.

—George Eliot

[IF I ONLY KNEW THEN WHAT I KNOW NOW™]

LESSON 156

YOU'RE NEVER TOO OLD

Live your life and forget your age.
—Frank Bering

Imagine that our planet was being visited by extraterrestrials who had never been here before, and their job was to come here, observe and report back home what they witnessed.

When the visitors returned home, they told their people, "These men and women on planet earth are really quite remarkable. They have a certain power that will allow them to achieve any goal they desire. But the strange thing is, the majority of them keep putting obstacles to their happiness in their way, sort of like self-sabotage. And one of the greatest observed was the excuse of 'being too old.'"

THE LESSON TO BE LEARNED IS...

You're only too old if you think you're too old, and there's nothing more to it than that.

"But you don't know my situation," you reply.

Excuses, excuses. They never stop.

First, it was that you were too young.

Then it was that you didn't have enough money.

Then came the excuse of not having enough time because you were working so much to make the money you told yourself you needed.

Then, when you had the money, you wanted to preserve it and not take any chances on losing it.

Then you had the money and had relieved any fears that you would lose it, but you felt it was too late to make anything of yourself or do the things you'd always wanted.

But I have one more excuse for you and it's going to be the final one…

Your life's meter has expired and it's time for you to go.

Oops… sorry.

My friend, you're never too old to do whatever it is you want.

It truly is never too late to be what you might have been.

LIFE'S WORDS OF WISDOM

Courage and perseverance have a magical talisman, before which difficulties disappear and obstacles vanish into air.

—John Quincy Adams

[IF I ONLY KNEW THEN WHAT I KNOW NOW™]

LESSON 157

DESIRE IS THE FORCE BEHIND ALL THINGS AND MOVES THE WORLD

*Be choosy, therefore, about what you set your heart on;
for if you want to achieve it strongly enough, you will.*
—Ashley Montagu

Everywhere you go, people have interests and lots of them. Variety is, after all, the spice of life. Wouldn't our lives be boring if we didn't have myriad interests?

But interests are one thing; desires are another.

The world moves and is changed by desire.

Desires—whether they be wise or unwise, positive or negative—are the things that become reality.

Desire fulfills a human need, a craving if you will, for something in each us that hungers to experience it.

Yet what most don't realize is that many of our desires come from past programming and emotion-backed demands that keep telling you that in order to feel happy, fulfilled, excited or complete, you must have these things or a person(s) who will give them to you.

And depending on how you look at it, the trouble is—or the great thing is—desire never stops.

THE LESSON TO BE LEARNED IS...

Whatever you desire can help you or hurt you.

Only you can say which.

For any choice you make or anything you set your mind to achieve or experience, there are consequences you must experience.

Look at your desires and ask yourself why you want the things you do.

Listen to the answers, for they will reveal a lot about why you've devoted so much of your life to chasing after the things you have.

Keep the fire of desire burning inside you.

It will change your life.

Having the right desire will change it for the best.

LESSON 158

YOUR ENVIRONMENT IMPACTS YOUR REALITY

Our life is what our thoughts make of it.
—Marcus Aurelius

Each environment you experience carries its own set of thoughts, feelings, beliefs and values.

Whether it be your job, home, gym, school, social gatherings or anything else, each can trigger things inside that cause you to think only in the certain ways you'd think when you're in that environment.

THE LESSON TO BE LEARNED IS...

You think, act, believe, perform and see yourself as different kind of person whenever you're around certain kinds of people and in certain kinds of environments.

Think back to various environments you've been in or are currently in and you'll see this is true.

The important thing to always remember is that the environment is neutral and causes you to do nothing that you haven't allowed yourself to think and accept.

It all begins with your perception of whatever it is you're experiencing.

You can change how your environment affects you by changing your thoughts towards it and how you perceive it.

Choose a new set of beliefs and attitudes that will empower you instead of taking your power away and causing you to feel unhappiness.

Create the reality you want by seeing and feeling yourself in the environment you choose.

:: The Lessons of Life and What They're Trying to Teach You ::

LESSON 159

WE REMEMBER MOST THOSE WHO WERE HARDEST ON US

I love you for what you are, but I love you more for what you are going to be. I love you not so much for your realities as for your ideals. I pray for your desires that they may be great, rather than for your satisfactions, which may be so hazardously little.

—Charles Sandburg

You know, many people are a lot like wagons; they don't want to go any further than they are pulled.

They seem to coast through life and never really do much with their lives or for others.

But don't we remember—even after all these years—the people came into our lives and made a difference?

Think of your coaches, teachers and friends who were hard on you and wouldn't let you accept second best, and how their influence to this day can still be felt.

They were the ones who saw the greatness in us, forced us to pull ourselves up by the bootstraps and expected nothing less than our best in whatever we did.

These are the people we remember.

THE LESSON TO BE LEARNED IS...

At the time we were going through it, we probably didn't think too highly of these hard-nosed disciplinarians. Where in the heck did they get off trying to tell us what to do! Oh, but don't you wish you had them now.

They brought something out of you that you didn't know you were capable of.

They held you up to a higher standard and by doing so made you—maybe for the first time in your life—hold yourself up to that higher standard of excellence.

That higher standard helped you achieve and experience what you never thought possible. And as result, you became a better person.

Isn't it amazing to think just how much you're still influenced in some way, even after all these years, by what these people did for you?

Now it's your turn to pass the torch and do it for someone else.

LIFE'S WORDS OF WISDOM

Obstacles in the pathway of the weak become stepping stones in the pathway of the strong.

—Thomas Carlyle

[IF I ONLY KNEW THEN WHAT I KNOW NOW™]

LESSON 160

LIFE IS MADE UP OF DEFINING MOMENTS

The tests of life are to make, not break us. Trouble may demolish a man's business but build his character. The blow at the outward man may be the greatest blessing to the inner man. If God, then, puts or permits anything hard in our lives, be sure that the real peril, the real trouble, is what we shall lose if we flinch or rebel.
—Maltbie D. Babcock

Defining moments or words are those things that change people's lives and destiny forever.

A decision you've been putting off, an unexpected event that forces you to make a decision and take a course of action. All these and others can, at the time, seem so tough to go through, like you want to throw your arms up in the air and give up.

But that something inside you didn't let you quit or back away from the decisions you knew you had to make.

THE LESSON TO BE LEARNED IS...

Welcome any and all defining moments in your life, because many times that's the only way God can get through your thick head the direction you need to go and the thoughts you now need to be thinking.

Just like well-intentioned friends who see the impending collision—what's going to happen to you unless you change some things in your life—many times before you do, your Creator has a perfect plan and direction for your life if only you'll be still and listen.

:: The Lessons of Life and What They're Trying to Teach You ::

The truly successful have always followed that course of action, much like the following from J. L. Kraft, one of the real giant successes in business and in life: "When I have a problem I pray about it, and what comes to mind and stays there I assume to be my answer. And this has been right so often that I know it is God's answer."

All defining moments help you to grow; never do they take away from what you were meant to be.

Look for them.

Ask for awareness to understand them.

Every day, you'll find a defining a moment that can change your life.

[IF I ONLY KNEW THEN WHAT I KNOW NOW™]

LESSON 161

BE HARD ON YOURSELF AT THE RIGHT TIME

He who would do some great thing in this short life, must apply himself to the work with such a concentration of his forces as to idle spectators, who live only to amuse themselves, looks like insanity.
—John Foster

Inside you right now is a deep need for you to be pushed to your limits.

This need, like many others, must be tempered, for too much of one thing leads to an imbalance of others.

Life is short. And for you to achieve any measure of greatness, you must listen to that inner desire to stretch yourself beyond the comfort level you've been so used to and climb to a higher level of experience.

THE LESSON TO BE LEARNED IS...

Pushing yourself to expand your possibilities and life's experiences is a tremendous growing experience. And one of the best ways to prove that to yourself is by working out. You will be astonished at how your body will look and feel after only 30 days of hard training and eating healthy.

But guess what? Working out is not the only way you can push yourself.

Sometimes employers push us positively and beyond anything we've ever done.

Sometimes friends and loved ones push you.

Yet, the real reward comes when you push yourself by yourself.

Don't wait for the perfect time or situation to push yourself. Each day, the clock of your life is ticking.

The time you waste today is the time you won't have tomorrow to enjoy all the incredible rewards you'll experience from pushing yourself beyond that which you've been.

| LIFE'S WORDS OF WISDOM |

Make not your thoughts your prisons.

—William Shakespeare

[IF I ONLY KNEW THEN WHAT I KNOW NOW™]

LESSON 162

TEAR DOWN YOUR FENCES

You shall know the truth and the truth shall set you free.
—John 8:32

You were born with only two fears: the fear of falling and the fear of loud noises.

Every other fear is learned.

Silly isn't it? Big, strong you, after all these years accepting so little of yourself and being so afraid to do something new or go after your dream.

Think about something with me for a moment.

When you were born, you had every possibility for becoming that which you want to be and doing that which you want to do. A life of unlimited possibility and greatness was yours.

Each year as you grew older (only in years), you began listening, believing and accepting without question the limits that your family, friends, co-workers and society placed on you and the future possibilities for your life.

These limits became your fences.

And each year, you accepted more and more of what these people told you. And as you did, those fences began to surround you and came gradually closer and closer to tightly fencing you in to where now, you can only go forward and backward for a few steps and that's all.

And after all these years, you've come to actually believe that these limits and imaginary fences are real for you, even though in reality they never existed except in your mind.

Yes, you were born with an ocean of possibilities—unlimited in abundance and impossible to see the end of it—but now the only ocean of possibilities you see for yourself is a small bucket with a little water.

It's time to throw the bucket away.

THE LESSON TO BE LEARNED IS…

The great news for you is that every single one of those dreams you had as a child and that ocean of unlimited possibilities have always been there for you and they're still there right now, waiting for you to push those fences over and enjoy them.

When it comes to having the kind of incredible life you want, it's never too early or too late to go for it.

Who cares what others think. For years, you've cared too much of what others thought, and look at how it's made you feel.

You were meant to have the kind of life you've always dreamed of.

Those dreams were placed inside you for a reason.

It's time to tear down your fences.

LIFE'S WORDS OF WISDOM

Every time a person admits to himself—usually much later—that he has made a fool of himself, he can trace it to a lack of patience; if he had only waited a while, everything would have been all right.

—Earl Nightingale

[IF I ONLY KNEW THEN WHAT I KNOW NOW™]

LESSON 163

SAY WHAT YOU WANT

Every day, in every way, I'm getting better and better.
—Émile Coué

You can be whatever you tell yourself you want to be, so why is it that you keep telling yourself what you are and what you don't want?

Your mind is the most powerful machine ever created and will bring you whatever you tell it to bring you, provided that you tell it enough times, back those commands with emotion, and tell it in the present tense, as if you've already achieved it.

But what do most people do?

They tell themselves what they don't want, what they can't do, who they can't be and why and so many other limiting beliefs.

Like these…

- "I can't…"
- "I'm so…"
- "I don't have…"
- "I won't…"
- "I'm too…"
- "I never…"
- "I wish I could…"
- "I know I should…"

- "I should've..."
- "I could've..."
- "I might have..."
- "I never..."
- "I always..."
- "I get so..."
- "That's unbelievable."
- "That's impossible."
- "I have a tough time at..."
- "I hate..."
- "If only I had more money, time, opportunities, knew the right people, were smarter, prettier, not so out of shape...."

Every single one of these are words and phrases you hear people use every single day, so is it any wonder they continue to keep being and experiencing all the things they keep telling themselves that they are, yet say they don't want to be?

THE LESSON TO BE LEARNED IS...

The things and experiences you have in your life today are to a very large degree, because you keep telling your mind who and what you are and what you can and cannot do.

Remember, your subconscious mind (the powerhouse that changes your life) listens to every single word you verbally or quietly tell yourself throughout the day.

And it never sleeps.

[IF I ONLY KNEW THEN WHAT I KNOW NOW™]

Its only job is to listen to what you tell yourself over and over and make those beliefs come true in your life.

You truly cannot and will not rise above your words.

Your words are incredibly powerful, so tell yourself only what you want to happen, what you want to be, and what you want to experience.

And make those affirmations in the present tense, like they are already happening.

Here's what I'm talking about…

- "I look and feel great."
- "I enjoy eating healthy foods and am always full of energy."
- "Incredible wealth, success and opportunities are flowing into my life right now."
- "I know exactly what I need to do at the perfect time, and I do it."
- "I am guided unerringly in all that I do, every day."

And one of the most powerful of all affirmations was the one that late Émile Coué gave to his patients that profoundly changed their lives:

- "Every day, in every way, I'm getting better and better."

Remember this:

- The experiences and words you heard helped create your beliefs.
- Those beliefs helped create your attitudes.
- Those attitudes helped create your feelings.

- Those feelings helped you decide what actions you'll take.
- The actions you've taken have given you the results you've experienced.
- Always say the best words to yourself.

Really believe what you say, even though at this moment, it may be the furthest thing from the truth.

For soon it will be true, if only you'll say whatever it is you want.

LESSON 164

THE IMAGES YOU KEEP PLAYING IN YOUR MIND KEEP BRINGING YOU THE THINGS YOU HAVE

All day, every day, you speak in words, but think in images and pictures.

This is what our ancestors did when they didn't have the language we now have.

They drew pictures on walls, in caves, in the dirt, on wood. Each image had a specific meaning.

The same is true today.

The problem is, most people picture in their minds that which they want to avoid. Very few vividly picture that which they want. But when they do, they find themselves irresistibly drawn to it, as if something magical is happening.

Well, something magical *is* happening.

They're using their mind the way it is meant to be used.

As a life-changing, goal-achieving machine that will bring them whatever they truly desire, if only they'll keep the image burning vividly in their mind.

THE LESSON TO BE LEARNED IS…

Want to change your life and experience the things you deeply want?

:: The Lessons of Life and What They're Trying to Teach You ::

Simply change the image and pictures that you constantly think about.

See vividly and clearly, with as much detail as possible, those new things you want.

Let the incredible new emotions of having and experiencing whatever it is you want fill your mind, and feel the warmth and goose bumps all over your body.

These feelings will definitely happen. And when they do, you can be assured that some powerful changes are going on inside you, and those changes will take you in a hurry to whatever it is you desire.

| LIFE'S WORDS OF WISDOM |

A great many people think they are thinking when they are merely rearranging their prejudices.

—William James

[IF I ONLY KNEW THEN WHAT I KNOW NOW™]

LESSON 165

TIME TO CLEAN OUT THE CLOSET

Beliefs are like old clothes; you need to regularly get rid of the ones you don't need.

Think about some of your beliefs.

Have they helped you or held you back?

Made you miserable or happy? Frustrated or fulfilled?

For most of us, those beliefs were formed without much thought. After all, we like to feel comfortable and have an answer or belief for just about any experience we may come across.

THE LESSON TO BE LEARNED IS…

Just like old clothes, you need to clean out your belief closet—your mind—on a regular basis.

Keep the ones you like to wear, those beliefs that help you grow and experience love and happiness, those that expand your awareness for all the possibilities for greatness that lie within you and help you achieve your goals and dreams.

You have permission to throw away the rest.

[IF I ONLY KNEW THEN WHAT I KNOW NOW™]

LESSON 166

THE INCREDIBLE POWER OF ONE

One person, one voice, one vote and one action can make all the difference and even change the world.
—Anonymous

We live in a country in which, despite the horrendous price for freedom men and women paid before we were born, we hardly take full advantage of our liberties and exercise the greatest power that was ever to be bestowed upon us.

I'm talking about the power to vote.

But it goes way beyond just voting.

It's the power of one.

That's right, one person, one voice, once cause and one action that can change the world.

Most people still live with the belief that what they do or what they say couldn't be that important.

But they are wrong.

Take a good look at what the power of one did to change the course of history:

- In 1645, one vote gave Oliver Cromwell control of England.

- In 1649, one vote caused Charles I of England to be executed.

- In 1776, one vote gave America the English language instead of German.

- In 1845, one vote brought Texas into the Union.

- In 1868, one vote saved President Andrew Johnson from impeachment.

- In 1876, one vote gave Rutherford B. Hayes the presidency of the United States.

- In 1923, one vote gave Adolf Hitler leadership of the Nazi Party.

The point is, anyone can make a difference in changing the course of events in their lives and for those people around them. We think that we can't change laws in this country, yet, many powerful politicians say that isn't so.

So few people write or call them to express their views that the silence of the majority is taken by these politicians to mean that everyone is happy with the way things are going. No wonder these same politicians tend to listen more to those few who do call or write.

THE LESSON TO BE LEARNED IS...

Your voice, your ideas and your beliefs are just as important as those of anyone else, regardless of their money, power or prestige. Power is simply something we give somebody else because we choose to. Just as easily, you can take it away.

It all begins with you, the power of one.

[IF I ONLY KNEW THEN WHAT I KNOW NOW™]

LESSON 167

JUST GET IN THE NEIGHBORHOOD

The more I believe I will reach my goal, the less I need to know how. The more I think about having already arrived at my goal, the quicker I actually get there.

So many times, people can't decide what they want to do with their lives, and it stops them from ever taking action or experiencing in the first place.

They want to know the exact steps they'll take and what might happen along the way on the road to their dreams and goals.

Life doesn't work that way.

This is precisely the reason these same people will never change their lives and do something different. The fear of not knowing is much greater than the happiness of experiencing and achieving.

Can I let you in on a little secret?

You simply don't need to know exactly how, when and where things will happen. In all probability, it will end up being way different from what you first imagined.

You just need to get in the neighborhood.

THE LESSON TO BE LEARNED IS...

When deciding what you want to do with your life and which direction you should go, all you need to do is just get in the vicinity and the rest will become crystal clear.

:: The Lessons of Life and What They're Trying to Teach You ::

Realize that whatever you do, your first experience will not be your final experience.

Knowing that takes the pressure off you and helps you to understand that it's not a big deal if only you get in the neighborhood, so to speak, the first time out.

Here's what being in the vicinity of what you think you want to do, will do.

For years, you may have dreamed that only being an actor will bring you your greatest happiness. So, you get a job at a studio as a production assistant and in a short time, you find that the politics, the hours and the people weren't anything like you imagined it would be all those years. You may also find out that the passion for acting may not be as strong as you once thought it was.

But in a few short weeks or months, look what you've learned. And look at how much time and possible headache that you've saved.

And it's all because you were in the vicinity.

Do that for anything and everything in your life and you'll be amazed at the time, energy, emotion, effort and money you'll save along the way.

| LIFE'S WORDS OF WISDOM |

When love and skill work together, expect a masterpiece.

—John Ruskin

[IF I ONLY KNEW THEN WHAT I KNOW NOW™]

LESSON 168

DO THE THINGS YOU WANT TO DO

*Destiny is not a matter of chance;
it is a matter of choice.
It is not a thing to be waited for;
it is a thing to be achieved.*

—William Jennings Bryan

"It's not what I really want to do, but the experience will look good on my résumé."

Have you ever heard anyone say that?

I can't begin to count the number of people who have told me this as they continued to accept second best for their life and kept their mind off really deciding what they wanted.

A résumé is a piece of paper. That's all.

You can have the best grades in school, do the most extra-curricular activities, go to the best school and graduate with honors, and you will be in the company of many others just like you, all looking for those same opportunities.

THE LESSON TO BE LEARNED IS...

If you think graduating from college is your ticket to the good life, think again. The only thing you can be sure of if you have a college degree is that you have a college degree. That's all, folks.

Picture this scenario and you'll see what I mean.

You're the owner of a company. Two people come in to see you for a job, and you ask them, during their appointments, to tell you something about themselves. The first applicant says, "Well, I'm a self-starter and highly motivated and a real people person. I graduated with honors from a famous (and expensive) Ivy League University, and I was captain of the volleyball team, president of the honor society, editor of the school newspaper and president of the marketing clubs. I also worked two jobs to pay my way through school. I know I would be perfect for the job."

The second person arrives and in response to your question says, "Well, Mr./Ms. Business Owner, I've done quite a bit of research about your company and found some key niche markets that you haven't tapped.

"In fact, neither have any of your competitors, and your product would be the perfect fit for this untapped goldmine of opportunity. I've put together a list of 15 different money-making, wealth-producing, market-specific ideas that will immediately increase your market share and public awareness of your company. May I share those with you?"

Share them?

This person would be my top candidate, and I'd bet they'd be yours too.

The first thing they did to separate themselves from everyone else out there is they thought of my business first.

They didn't have to tell me about themselves.

Their actions said everything I needed to know to put them on the road to the brass ring.

The point here is that college is wonderful for those for whom it is right. Besides knowledge, probably the most important thing it teaches is the discipline to keep on learning.

Yet only if you apply what you've learned to the real world and that career area/vicinity that excites you, will you ever be the real success you were meant to be.

Remember, when you start developing the talents and gifts that are uniquely your own, you will quickly learn that you have no competition. In fact, competition is a big misconception, because no one can do what you can do the way you do it.

So don't you dare compare yourself to anyone else.

And that résumé?

A wiser course of action for you would be to spend your time creating great ideas and services that will benefit people that fully use the gifts, talents and incredible abilities that are uniquely your own.

Be your own boss.

That's one of the best ways to predict and control your future and have the kind of life and lifestyle you dream of.

Never forget that the more service you provide to others, the greater will be your reward, and it won't be long until you're the business owner getting résumés.

| LIFE'S WORDS OF WISDOM |

Ideals are like stars: you will not succeed in touching them with your hands, but like the seafaring man on the desert of waters, you choose them as your guides, and, following them, you reach your destiny.

—Carl Shurz

[IF I ONLY KNEW THEN WHAT I KNOW NOW™]

LESSON 169

PLAN YOUR DREAMS ON WHAT YOU WANT AND NOT ON WHAT YOU HAVE

If we worked on the assumption that what is accepted as true, really is true, there'd be little hope of advance.
—Orville Wright

One of the hardest things for people to understand is to dream their dreams and plan their future on what they want and not on what they currently have.

It's easy to see why they do what they do.

After all, it's much easier to plan your life around your current income and most familiar experiences, especially those that have become your daily grind.

But if you keep doing what you're doing, you'll keep having what you're having.

THE LESSON TO BE LEARNED IS...

When you look back, in order to make any significant changes in your life, you had to first raise the expectancy of your goals and dreams and elevate them to the level of what you wanted and not what you had.

Usually, it's the pain of continually going through an unpleasant situation that forces you to break out of the chains that have held you in one place for so long. Your new way of thinking, along with new dreams and goals, put you on the happiness road and eventually lead you to a new and better place.

But only allowing your life to change whenever the pain becomes too unbearable is a waste of your precious time and life.

It doesn't have to be that way at all.

Right now, start thinking of the things you'd really love to have and experience, and the kind of person you'd most like to become.

Forget about putting any limits on yourself.

Right now, I want you to think about what it is you would most want if time, money, age, education and anything else weren't factors.

Really feel what it would feel like to experience these things right now, not in some imagined distant future that never quite seems to get here.

I want you to act like this is the only day you have to live, and you will do only the things you'd most like to experience.

As you begin doing this, the pictures that you'll send to your mind will begin to take hold of every fiber of your being and fill you with such incredible feelings that you'll wish you'd done this years ago.

That's okay.

The most important thing is that you're doing it now; and right now, you've begun to change your life, the way you want it to be and for the incredible best.

:: The Lessons of Life and What They're Trying to Teach You ::

LESSON 170

GO TO THE WATER FOR CLEANSING

Most of man's trouble comes from his inability to be still.
—Blaise Pascal

What is it about water that makes it so calming to the soul?

Clear liquid, nothing more, yet, just being around it can quiet even the most turbulent of lives and open our hearts and souls to the message that waits deep inside.

Water. Shapeless, formless and powerful.

For eons, men and women have sought to hear it, be near it, and in it.

Like air, it's the very stuff we're made of.

THE LESSON TO BE LEARNED IS...

Do you really want to rid those angers, hurts, fears and frustrations and make perfect peace with yourself to reach your greatest success and happiness?

Then go to the water.

And do it regularly.

All you need to do is just sit near it and listen.

Ask yourself which things are bothering you.

The answer will come. And when it does, forgive whoever may have hurt you and remember the lesson and throw away the experience by casting all those hurts out to sea.

Feel your body and soul being cleansed and the storms of your life calming.

Become like the rocks.

For every time the waves of life crash against and cover them, they become washed clean and new again as the waves go back out to sea.

See your life like that.

And always know that even though you may have been and are still going through some difficult and hard times, just like the rocks that are constantly washed by the sea, so will the storms of your life calm and your soul be cleansed.

LIFE'S WORDS OF WISDOM

When a person finds himself, when he stops imitating and envying others, there is something in his nature that says to him, "This is it. You've found your road at last."

—Earl Nightingale

[IF I ONLY KNEW THEN WHAT I KNOW NOW™]

LESSON 171

WHY BE A COPY WHEN YOU CAN BE THE ORIGINAL?

Will you be the one who devotes a lifetime to talking or writing about someone else's life, or will people talk and write about yours?

Amazing isn't it? Most people spend a great deal of their conversation talking about the lives of other people instead of making theirs a life that others will talk about and remember.

In a world of billions of people, why have we become so obsessed with copying the way others look, act and believe?

Why do we believe their accomplishments are always more important than our own?

Why do we insist on being a copy when we are an original?

THE LESSON TO BE LEARNED IS...

Few people ever remember who the best man or maid of honor or second place finisher is.

Even fewer care.

People remember and are impacted by those special people who are different from the masses.

Those who decided to allow their real personalities, gifts, talents and abilities to come out and do what they dream instead of dreaming dreams that never leave the inside of their head.

You are just as special, unique and different as your favorite movie or music star. Your name can just as easily be in lights, in the newspaper, in magazines, on television, on the radio, in books and records and in the movies, if that's what you truly desire.

Life is so short.

Look at how fast it's gone so far. And I've got news for you: The coming years will fly by even faster.

Now is the time to let go of the belief that someday you'll definitely do what you've always dreamed of.

That someday is now, my friend.

The world is waiting to see you, the true original.

LIFE'S WORDS OF WISDOM

Wait patiently for the Lord. God is never in a hurry. Then when He speaks to you—as He will—do what He tells you. It generally comes through your own conscience—a sort of growing conviction that such and such a course of action is the one He wants you to take.
Or it may be given you in advice of friends of sound judgment—those who love you most. God speaks sometimes through our circumstances and guides us, closing doors as well as opening them.

—Peter Marshall

[IF I ONLY KNEW THEN WHAT I KNOW NOW™]

LESSON 172

NEVER RUSH GOD'S TIMING AND HIS PLAN FOR YOUR LIFE

Lord of Lords, grant us the good whether we pray for it or not, but evil keep from us, even though we pray for it.
—Plato

The world is filled with people who want to control every aspect of their lives and must see every step they'll take—and what will happen along the way—before they'll take action, feel happy and let go.

Yet they never let go.

It's not that they can't; they simply won't.

THE LESSON TO BE LEARNED IS...

Deny all you want to, but you were created by a power much greater than you.

And wouldn't it just make perfect sense if that same power—your Creator—also made you, knowing exactly what you needed at any point in your life, and was ready at any time to give it to you, but with one pre-condition?

Timing.

It comes down to trusting God's plan and *timing* for your life. Sorry, friend, but operate on your schedule is not something this incredible power source will do.

Good thing.

| LIFE'S WORDS OF WISDOM |

The passions are the only orators that always persuade; they are, as it were, a natural art the rules of which are infallible; and the simplest man with passion is more persuasive than the most eloquent without it.

—Francois de La Rochefoucauld

LESSON 173

ALWAYS HAVE PASSION AND ROMANCE FOR EVERYTHING YOU DO

When you love what you do, you'll never work another day in your life.

—Anonymous

Care to count how many lifeless souls you see every day? I tell you, it's like an epidemic, all the frowns, sad faces and blank stares. It's as if life were a prison sentence handed out at birth, and the rest of their lives are the prison they must be caged in.

Whatever happened to the passion and enthusiasm that each of us has—passion and enthusiasm that can turn any life from one of boredom to one filled with excitement?

All we have to do is simply choose to use them.

Boring people lead boring lives, and they do so by choosing to think boring thoughts and holding onto the same old worn-out dreams that keep giving them the same old results, day in and day out, year after boring year after boring year.

Time to wake up and smell the opportunities.

THE LESSON TO BE LEARNED IS...

The people we admire most are those who live life with passion, enthusiasm and love for people and what they do.

They realize that by following their dreams, they are doing what they love to do and are richly rewarded for it.

[IF I ONLY KNEW THEN WHAT I KNOW NOW™]

They are the ones who have reached the road of happiness in life.

Find your passion in life and follow it. As Joseph Campbell would say, "Follow your bliss."

Don't accept what you like only second or third best, or what you think you should be doing.

The only thing you should be doing is living life the way you want and making it pay off on your own terms.

Only then will you feel the passion that will change your life forever and make you great.

| LIFE'S WORDS OF WISDOM |

Great men are like rivers; the deepest and most powerful are always the quietest.

—Baltasar Gracian

[IF I ONLY KNEW THEN WHAT I KNOW NOW™]

LESSON 174

BE STILL AND LISTEN

What the inner voice says will not disappoint the hoping soul.

—Johann Christoph Friedrich von Schiller

Why do people think they have to be so busy and doing something all the time?

Who said that happiness and the quality and purpose of one's life are directly related to how busy they are?

Why have tension, stress, headaches, muscle spasms, lack of sleep, missed meals, poor nutrition and digestion and lack of exercise become the prerequisites for a life of too much busyness?

And that's only the start...

THE LESSON TO BE LEARNED IS...

The only way you can hear that still small voice within you that wants to guide you, is to be still and listen.

You can't hear it with the music jamming in your ear with earbuds in and smartphone on.

And you certainly will never hear it if your life must be filled with such busyness that even 10 minutes of being still seems like torture.

It's time you started treating yourself better. You deserve it. It's time to stop punishing yourself by thinking that your worth of who you are as a person depends upon how busy you are.

The greatest minds and people have always been those who taken time each day to find quiet moments throughout the day and listen what their intuition tells them.

Silence is power, and those precious moments of silence each day will fill you with a power that will, without fail, give you unerring guidance to where you need to go and what you need to do.

And if you're quiet, you can hear it now.

[IF I ONLY KNEW THEN WHAT I KNOW NOW™]

LESSON 175

CHANGE YOUR EXPECTATIONS TO PREFERENCES

The mind is its own place, and in itself can make a heaven of hell, a hell of heaven.
—John Milton

You couldn't even begin to count how many people will be frustrated today because their expectations are not met regarding how they think something should happen.

Yet haven't we all felt like that at some point in our lives? The feelings of being drained and let down—not so much by others, but rather by our rigidity and demands—that life and the events it contains do not conform to the way we want them to.

There is a better way.

THE LESSON TO BE LEARNED IS...

I want you to do something that will dramatically change how you look at things; it will take the pressure off you and give you more happiness and growth. Best of all, you can do it right now.

First, in your mind, begin to change your expectations to preferences.

Expectations mean that for you to be truly happy, things must happen in a certain way by a certain time. Let go of those expectations and simply prefer that they would happen that way. The difference will be astounding.

When you prefer that things happen, you take the pressure off yourself and allow yourself to be open to all the new possibilities and experiences you could not have when you were expecting them to happen a certain way.

And who said that your way of expecting things to happen was and is the best way for those things to happen, anyhow?

When you expect, you are merely using your limited frame of reference based on your past experiences and what you've read and heard from others in order to formulate your judgment that what you know is the very best for you.

If you believe there is a Creator and that things are fashioned not by chance or accident, you can then plainly see that your higher purpose and direction for your life—and the events and the lives of others—is an incredible, well-thought-out plan that will unfold to you once you let go of the expectations.

Once you see and feel the results, it'll be something you'll prefer.

| LIFE'S WORDS OF WISDOM |

God can do great things through the person who doesn't care who gets the credit.

—Anonymous

[IF I ONLY KNEW THEN WHAT I KNOW NOW™]

LESSON 176

A PREVIEW OF WHAT HAPPPENS AS YOU BEGIN LIVING YOUR NEW LIFE

*If a man will begin with certainties,
he shall end in doubts;
but if he will be content to begin with doubts,
he shall end in certainties.*
—Francis Bacon

One of the hardest things about living a new kind of life is allowing yourself to accept it.

Dreaming of a new life is easy and fun, because all you're doing is dreaming. Yet as you dream long enough and with powerful emotion behind those dreams, things inside you begin to change. You feel pulled to those dreams, and now your mind becomes obsessed with finding ways to make those dreams come true.

This is a huge deal for most people, for the majority of them never leave the dreaming step.

For those who do, their lives will never be the same, if only they'll stay on the road and not get freaked out when the inevitable begins to happen...

THE LESSON TO BE LEARNED IS...

The first thing that happens is doubt.

As you begin to change, your mind will present to you—of course, at the strangest times—doubt.

After all, you've lived your life this way for so long and now you're telling your brain you want to change. Doubt is your mind's way of saying "Are you sure this is something you really want to do?"

Of course it is.

You're sick and tired of being sick and tired.

At the same time doubt begins to surface, you begin to understand that for you to ever be financially independent, have your own business or do whatever it is you've always dreamed of doing each day, you have to give yourself permission to change your daily schedule, even if it's only one little step at a time.

Again, this may be hard at first because of the way you've lived your life in the past. If you've always worked an 8-to-5 job somewhere for years and now you have the opportunity to work at home, it's going to feel weird—at least at first.

Once you get into the groove of your new schedule, you're going to love it!

Guaranteed.

You might be afraid, though, wondering, "What if I don't make it?"

Or you might be wondering, "Will I be disciplined enough to keep doing the things I've always told myself I could do?"

But now that time has actually arrived, and you're going to have to do them.

Understand that the doubt and fear signals are only protection mechanisms from your past programming of accepting the old lifestyle for so long.

Nothing more.

:: The Lessons of Life and What They're Trying to Teach You ::

Fear comes from the belief that you're powerless to change things in your life.

But now you know that it just isn't true.

As you get flowing into your new schedule, your mind will want to set up some kind of structure.

This can be good, as structure gives us boundaries—the right kind that can guide and focus our efforts more powerfully—and it seems to be human nature to desire to have some kind of boundaries.

Just be careful not to put too much rigidity and structure in your life.

This can cause you to feel frustrated due to the need to control every aspect of your life, when it's far more rewarding to enjoy life when you give up much of the unnecessary need for control.

Always remember that as you grow, you'll never change things in life until you quit trying to fit new ideas, concepts and experiences into your existing structure that says this is what you must have or do in order to enjoy life.

New things need new schedules.

Always keep yours open and ready to change.

LIFE'S WORDS OF WISDOM

*What lies behind you and
what lies in front of you,
pales in comparison
to what lies inside of you.*

—Ralph Waldo Emerson

[IF I ONLY KNEW THEN WHAT I KNOW NOW™]

LESSON 177

THE WALK WITH GOD

Knock and He'll open the door. Vanish and He'll make you shine like the sun. Fall and He'll raise you to the heavens. Become nothing and He'll turn you into everything.
—Rumi

Let me tell you a story about you and your life.

One day, after your life is finished here on this earthly plane, you meet God.

On that special day, He puts his arm around you and says, "C'mon, let's take a walk. I want you to tell me about your life."

As both of you begin walking down the road of heaven, you notice there are many open fields, all filled with many different things.

Contained in each field are replays, pictures and feelings of experiences, heartaches and hurts, joys and happiness of everything anyone has ever experienced in their lives.

As both of you continue walking, God suddenly stops and says to you, "Look out there. "

You look.

It's your field!

And it's filled with everything you ever experienced in your life. Oh, what memories it brings back!

God looks at you and says, "Tell me what you see."

"Well, God," you answer, "It's my life."

God smiles as he says, "So, why don't you tell me about it."

With your head held high, you look out in the field and speak.

"I think I had a pretty good life, God. I tried to do the right thing and treat people well. I had my share of failures, but just as many, if not more, successes.

"Sure, there were lots of heartaches and frustrations and things that happened that I never quite understood, but I did the best I could to figure them out, learn from them and move on. I had a good job, friends and family, so I think I did pretty well; don't you think so too, God?"

He smiles and puts his arm back around you and says, "C'mon, let me show you something up ahead."

Both of you begin walking again.

Up ahead you notice something incredible.

There, in front of you, is a field like you've never seen before. In this field are joy, happiness, love, deep fulfillment and meaning like you've never experienced before.

But that's only the beginning.

In that same field are also riches, opulence and abundance unlike anything you've ever dreamed of.

And it doesn't end there.

Among all those riches are opportunities overflowing and the most phenomenal feelings of success and growth like you never thought possible.

You pick up your jaw and with eyes open wide you look at God and gush, "Wow! I've never seen anything as incredible as this. What is this, God?"

:: The Lessons of Life and What They're Trying to Teach You ::

God looks at you with a loving smile and then looks out in the field as he answers, "Why that's the field I had made especially for you. If only you'd had more faith and belief in yourself, in your dreams and the gifts I gave you to bless others and yourself, and had more faith in Me to show you the way to achieve and experience everything in it. All your life I wanted it to be yours. Yes, I was always ready to give it to you, if only you had believed just a little more in yourself."

THE LESSON TO BE LEARNED IS...

You've already learned it.

[IF I ONLY KNEW THEN WHAT I KNOW NOW™]

SHARE YOUR FAVORITE LIFE LESSON STORY WITH THE WORLD

If you have a Life Lesson story about you, your family or friends, or a favorite Life Lesson you may have heard, please send it to us and we might choose it to be in our next book.

Go to www.RobertWolff.com and click on the **Tell Me Your Story** tab for all the details.

Thank You and Best Wishes!

www.ingramcontent.com/pod-product-compliance
Lightning Source LLC
Chambersburg PA
CBHW032028150426
43194CB00006B/198